H. Walniel

Jon Jones
Outside The Cage

Foreword

In the first volume of the mini-book series, MMA Fighters, **Outside The Cage & Behind Bars**, I introduced a legend in the making: professional mixed martial arts fighter Jon *Bones* Jones.

Some of you have told me and still reckoned that I was harsh, cruel and wrong when I referred to him as the best con artist in the MMA world.

To be clear, I did not imply in any way that Jones wins his fights by deceiving his opponent. The comparison came for the most part from his words and actions. Both are rarely aligned and too often contradictory.

But, before diving further into the reasons why I stand by my position about the amazing (in good and bad) Jon *Bones* Jones, let us review his troubled history inside and outside the cage:

- December 2008:
  - He is involved in car accident in New York

- January 2009:
  - He is involved in a second car accident in New York
  - His fiancée and newborn daughter are both in the car at the time of collision; they are uninjured
  - The Police cites Jones for "*unsafe passing*"

- December 2009:
  - He is disqualified for using illegal elbows during his bout against Matt Hamill at The Ultimate Fighter: Heavyweights Finale

- January 2011:
  - He is involved in another car accident in New Mexico

- March 2011:
    - With his trainers, Greg Jackson and Mike Winkeljohn, hours prior to the biggest fight of his young career, the main event of UFC 128 against Mauricio Rua for the UFC Light Heavyweight Championship belt, he successfully subdues a robber
    - He walks out of his bout with Mauricio Rua with the victory and the UFC Light Heavyweight title

- November 2011:
    - He is charged for driving with a suspended license by the Albuquerque Police Department and loss of traction
    - His car is towed away from the scene

- March 2012:
    - The charges for driving with a suspended license are dismissed due to failure to prosecute; i.e.: the District Attorney's office did not present the charges within the allowed 60 days

- May 2012:
    - He drives his Bentley into a telephone pole in Binghamton, New York while two women other than his wife are present in the car with him
    - The Police charges him with Driving While Intoxicated (DWI)

- June 2012:
    - He pleads guilty to DWI
    - He is fined $1,000
    - His driver's license is suspended for six months

- September 2012:
    - Dan Henderson pulls out from his bout against Jones at UFC 151 due to a partial rupture of his Medial Collateral Ligament

- ⬇ Jones is presented long time middleweight middle Chael Sonnen as replacement and refuses
- ⬇ UFC 151 is cancelled

- August 2014:
  - ⬇ While promoting UFC 178, during the traditional pre-fight stare-down, he is involved in the now infamous brawl with Daniel Cormier in the sin city of Las Vegas

- September 2014:
  - ⬇ He is given a $50,000 fine and 40 hours of community service for his brawl with Daniel Cormier

- December 2014:
  - ⬇ He is tested positive for benzoylecgonine, the primary metabolite of cocaine
  - ⬇ He enters rehab
  - ⬇ He leaves rehab after only one day

- January 2015:
  - ⬇ He is fined $25,000 for violating the UFC's Athlete Code of Conduct policy after testing positive to cocaine

- April 2015:
  - ⬇ He is involved in a three-car accident in Albuquerque, NM.
  - ⬇ He flees the scene without checking on the other drivers, including a pregnant woman who broke her arm
  - ⬇ He runs back to his car to grab the cash that was in the car
  - ⬇ Police finds Marijuana, Marijuana pipe, and condoms in his car
  - ⬇ He is stripped of his title

- September 2015:

- ⬇ He avoids jail time by pleading guilty to charges stemming from his April 2015 hit-and-run
- ⬇ He is sentenced to serve 72 weeks of probation
- ⬇ He is also ordered to make 72 public speaking appearances to local youth

- January 2016:
  - ⬇ He is caught driving 75 miles per hour in a 35-mile-per-hour zone in Albuquerque, New Mexico
  - ⬇ He avoids a reckless driving traffic violation
  - ⬇ He is ticketed for driving without a license, registration or proof of insurance

- March 2016:
  - ⬇ He avoids charges for probation violation with only a $100 donation to charity and stipulations of not receiving any further citations for the next 90 days
  - ⬇ He enters the very next day in a heated argument with a Police Officer Brown after being pulled over for allegedly drag racing
  - ⬇ He is arrested for probation violation.
  - ⬇ He spends more than 48 hours in an Albuquerque jail cell waiting for the review of the terms of his probation

- April 2016:
  - ⬆ He wins his UFC return against Ovince Saint Preux
  - ⬆ He wins the interim UFC Light Heavyweight Championship

- June 2016:
  - ⬇ He is tested positive for the presence of hydroxyclomiphene (a metabolite of clomiphene) and a letrozole metabolite, a performance enhancement drug;

- July 2016:

- ⬇ He is removed for UFC 200 card for his failed drug test

- November 2016
  - ⬇ He avoids jail time by settling with the court about his March 2016 drag-racing charges
  - ⬇ He is sentenced to an additional 60 hours of community service and ordered to complete an aggressive driving course
  - ⬇ He is stripped of his interim title

- December 2016:
  - ⬇ He is suspended a year for his pre-fight UFC200 failed drug test

For someone who has never stop depicting himself countless times as "*a religious guy,*" as "*a Christian,*" it's hard to comprehend how his behavior and actions relate to his lengthy-publically discussed faith and values.

Visibly, undeniably, there is a gap; a humongous gap!

But, as we all know and understand, everyone deserves a second chance; and at times, a third or fourth chance. And so, in this mini-book, even though I do discuss into great details Jon *Jones's* troubled history outside the cage and behind bars, taking a few harsh stands on his actions, I am hopeful we can all keep an open-mind.

Let's indeed give the fighter a chance to prove everyone wrong, one day, and one fight at a time.

Table of Contents

Foreword iii
Disclaimer xi
Table of Figures xiii
1   Twelve Steps 1
2   Rise and Fame 1
3   Win and Lie 7
4   Catch and Pretend 21
5   Talk and Feud 27
6   Reveal and Cry 29
    6.1   Positive on Cocaine 29
    6.2   Hit-and-Run Charges 31
    6.3   Drag-Racing Charges 41
    6.4   Anti-Doping Policy Violation 49
7   Talk and… 53
For More Information 59
    References 59
    Photo Credits 62
    Appendices 63
        Appendix 1: Jon Jones's January 2011 Police Report 64
        Appendix 2: Jon Jones's April 2015 Hit-and-Run Police Report 66
        Appendix 3: Jon Jones's April 2015 Arrest Warrant Affidavit 73
        Appendix 4: Jon Jones's November 2016 Arbitration Ruling 75
From the Author 105

Disclaimer

This book contains detailed information about extremely violent crimes committed in recent years, and describes the actual crime scenes that some readers may find disturbing. Reader discretion is advised.

This information is provided and sold with the knowledge that the author, editor and publisher do not acknowledge the discussed violent crimes.

Every effort has been made to make this book as accurate as possible. However, there may be typographical and or content errors. Therefore, this book should serve only as a general guide and not as the ultimate source of subject information.

This book contains information that might be dated and is intended only to educate and entertain. The author, editor, and publisher shall have no liability or responsibility to any person or entity regarding any loss or damage incurred, or alleged to have incurred, directly or indirectly, by the information contained in this book.

All suspects are innocent until proven guilty in a court of law.

You hereby agree to be bound by this disclaimer.

Table of Figures

Figure 1: Jackson, Jones, Winklejohn subdued a robber on March 2011 8
Figure 2: Jon Jones's car crash on May 2012 12
Figure 3: Jon Jones's May 2012 mugshot 13
Figure 4: Officer Martinez's November 2011 Report 15
Figure 5: Cara Johnson and Michelle Vojtisek 16
Figure 6: Jon Jones's May 2010 Tweet 25
Figure 7: Jon Jones's April 2015 Hit-and-Run Accident Diagram 33
Figure 8: Extract from the Jon Jones's Accident Police Report 35
Figure 9: Jon Jones's April 2015 Arrest Warrant 35
Figure 10: Albuquerque Police's April 2015 Tweet 36
Figure 11: Jon Jones's April 2015 mugshot 37
Figure 12: Jon Jones's March 24 2016 Police Camera Cam 44
Figure 13: Jon Jones's March 24 2016 Booking Information 45
Figure 14: Jon Jones's March 2016 mugshot 46
Figure 15: Jon Jones's March 2016 arraignment 46

1 Twelve Steps

Early 2016, Jon Jones admitted being an addict, and having dealt with alcohol and marijuana throughout his professional career.

Admission is the first step in the twelve steps of Alcoholic Anonymous. As we move forward, and look at Jon Bones Jones's next move, let's wish him success in his journey to recovery:

1. We admitted we were powerless over alcohol - that our lives had become unmanageable.
2. Came to believe that a Power greater than ourselves could restore us to sanity.
3. Made a decision to turn our will and our lives over to the care of God as we understood Him.
4. Made a searching and fearless moral inventory of ourselves.
5. Admitted to God, to ourselves and to another human being the exact nature of our wrongs.
6. Were entirely ready to have God remove all these defects of character.
7. Humbly asked Him to remove our shortcomings.
8. Made a list of all persons we had harmed, and became willing to make amends to them all.
9. Made direct amends to such people wherever possible, except when to do so would injure them or others.
10. Continued to take personal inventory and when we were wrong promptly admitted it.
11. Sought through prayer and meditation to improve our conscious contact with God as we understood Him, praying only for knowledge of His will for us and the power to carry that out.
12. Having had a spiritual awakening as the result of these steps, we tried to carry this message to alcoholics and to practice these principles in all our affairs.

2 Rise and Fame

In the first volume of the mini-book series, MMA Fighters, **Outside The Cage** & **Behind bars**, I may have been a little harsh, defining *Bones* as a thug. I guess, I was trying to be uncompromised and unforgiven.

Looking back, I was unambiguously too unforgiving. I was perhaps expecting much more from someone who showed so much promise inside the cage in his fairly young professional career.

That said, I do not regret this comparison as I do believe the definition of the word *thug* of the Urban Dictionary does apply well to Jones's pattern of behavior:

> *A low life criminal who believes that any crime or act of violence he or she commits to anyone or anything is perfectly acceptable behavior. As long as it's committed in the hopes of achieving something that he wants.*

I did and do continue admitting that Jones is without a doubt an intriguing and unavoidable character in MMA. As many other, fans or members of the press, I admired his rise to the Ultimate Fighting Championship (UFC) Light Heavyweight Title.

At the same time, I do realize that, while Jones was making his way to the title, I somehow eluded many details about his rise, and in particular his not-so-sportsmanship attitude inside the cage; i.e.: his DQ loss, and the numerous accidental eye-gauging incidents.

But, let's not go too fast in this story, and start where it all began, where it all began in the most genuine way…

Jonathan Dwight Jones was born on July 19, 1987 from Camille and Arthur Jr. Jones. He was raised in Rochester, New York, United States, which is, according to him, "*a pretty rough area to grow up in.*"

Growing up was not easy. His sister, Carmen, passed away in 2000 after a long 2-year battle against a brain cancer. As we would expect, having to deal with such tragic and unfair ordeal affected both his family and faith.

Jones had also no choice but to grow up faster than his peers. He had to support his family and her sister going through that heartbreaking battle. Unfortunately, at the age of 20 years old, she lost and passed away. This period was challenging for all his family, his parents, and his two brothers. They learned how to grief together and grow as a family.

His dad, a Pastor, helped the family in the grieving process, showing and demonstrating every day the importance and power of his faith, and the value of hard work.

Interviewed by Percy Crawford on September 8, 2008, a month after his successful first UFC bout, Jones shared with the reporter his personal background and his faith.

> "*When it comes to nerves, I'm a religious guy. I'm a Christian and a lot of my attitude and my confidence comes from me being a Christian. When I'm out there, I know that God is on my side and he's going to protect me and that he's not going to let anything too serious happen to me out there. I go out there and throw my hands and not really worry about what's going to happen to me.*"

In the *UFC Documentary: The Real Jon Jones,* prepared and released on April 18, 2012, days prior his bout against former teammate and rival Rashad Evans, at UFC 145: Jones vs. Evans, Jones candidly spoke about his early life, about his upbringing, about his family values and faith:

> "*I believe, religion, Christianity, is not for perfect people. It's for people who confessed they have issues and problems, and that they need a savior and that they need to work to be better. And, that's me.*"

In middle school and high-school, as many other kids, Jones liked playing various sports with his classmates, friends and brothers. But, he soon realized that he was a natural athlete.

Jones played football as a defensive lineman in high-school. This is where he inherited his nickname. Standing at 6 ft. 4 (193 cm), and weighting only 170 pounds (77 kg), his football coach named him *Bones* because of his long, lengthy and skinny frame. And, when he began his professional career, he kept the nickname, as a tribute to his high-school coaches.

However, Jones was not set on only one thing, on only one sport. He tried wrestling, starting "*in middle school and in high school.*" The sport seemed to fit him very well. He became a stand-out high school wrestler, and won the State Champion at the Union-Endicott High School in upstate New York.

After high-school, he went on to study at the Iowa Central Community College before transferring to Morrisville State College. And, then in April 11, 2008, at only 20 years old, Jones made the boldest decision, a decision that would drive him to success and fame. He dropped out of college, where he was studying Criminal Justice and began his MMA career.

And, his professional debut was nothing but fast and impressive. With only two months of MMA training, and after watching many online videos, he stepped into the cage for the first time against Brad *The Barroom Brawler* Bernard. One minute and thirty two seconds later, Jones had won the fight.

Seven days later, Jones went back into the cage. This time, he faced Carlos Eduardo, a veteran of 3 professional bouts. Jones would also win, knocking out his opponent in the third round. A tough fight in which the infant MMA skills of the fighter were tested. But, he managed and won.

Unstoppable, on April 25, 2008, he was ready for his third bout. No time to waste. After only 75 seconds, he once again won, submitting his opponent, Anthony Pina, by guillotine choke. In just six month, amazing Jones picked up 6 wins and the USKBA Light Heavyweight Championship.

And then, came the summer 2008. July. Jones received a call from the UFC.

Veteran Polish professional mixed martial artist Tomasz Drwal who was scheduled to face undefeated prospect André Gusmão at UFC 87 had to pull out of the bout due to a knee injury. Jones was called to replace the injured fighter. It did not wait for weighing the pros and cons. He jumped to the opportunity and agreed to replace Drwal on a two-week notice...

And when the day came, Jones was ready.

August 9, 2008. Minneapolis, Minnesota, United States. UFC 87.

A few days after his 21st birthday, Jones entered the octagon. 15 minutes later, when he stepped out, Jones had one more W. to add to his undisputed professional record. Unbreakable Jones.

Interviewed by reporter Percy Crawford on September 8, 2008, a month after his successful first UFC bout, the young gun, Jon *Bones* Jones shared his early life with the MMA world. He seemed genuine, candid, somehow naïve, and a virgin to any marketing campaign.

People, fans and members of the press, had no reason to doubt him, to challenge him. He was the new kid on the block.

His success and fame inside the cage continued. On January 31, 2009, he faced UFC Hall of Fame Stephan Bonnar, winning by decision after 3 hard-fought rounds. On July 11, 2009, at UFC 100, fighting in the preliminary card, he captured the win against veteran and former Heavyweight Jake O'Brien submitting him by an impressive modified guillotine choke.

He then experienced his first and only defeat on December 5, 2009, being disqualified for illegally elbowing a down-opponent. At the time, several news outlets and MMA fighters reckoned that Jones's DQ was unfair, and that he should have won the fight. But, a rule is a rule. Jones did throw an illegal elbow.

Jones would however rebound a few months later, easily winning to Brandon Vera by TKO (elbow and punches), and by the same token, earning his first Bonus Award, $50,000; Knockout of the Night.

On August 1, 2010, Jones added another win, defeating Vladimir Matyushenko, and on February 5, 2011, a twelfth victory, after submitting Ryan Bader at UFC 126.

Jones's beginning was nothing but extraordinary. And for displaying such amazing skills inside the cage, he was finally matched to fight for the gold, to fight for the UFC Light Heavyweight Championship Belt…

Jones had just turned 23 years old.

3   Win and Lie

On March 19, 2011, Jones entered the octagon to face legend and veteran Mauricio Rua. This was the most important fight in Jones's career. He was about to fight for the UFC Light Heavyweight Championship belt.

As the challenger, Jones was first to step into the cage. Mauricio then made his entrance. The rest belongs to the MMA and UFC history.

Bones won by TKO, defeating the legend and future Hall of Fame in an impressive manner: kneeing and punching Mauricio, winning by TKO 2 minutes and 37 seconds in the third round. That evening, he became de facto the youngest champion to capture the UFC Light Heavyweight title at the age of 23 years old.

The day did not go however as planned for the young fighter. Earlier that day, hours before the biggest fight of his career, Jones, and his trainers, Greg Jackson and Mike Winklejohn, had an interesting encounter…

They were going to Patterson, New Jersey to prepare for the fight ahead and mediate. While driving there, Glenn, one of Jones's co-managers, explained to the 3 men that the area was near a dangerous neighborhood, a neighborhood where people often get mugged.

As they prepared to get out of the car, and Glenn told them to be careful, they heard someone screaming. Jones looked back and saw an old Spanish couple running toward them. Mike Winklejohn stepped outside the car and asked them what happened and if they were okay. The woman explained him that a guy just broke her car-window opened and stole all her stuff. And, then, just like that, without hesitation, Mike Winklejohn began running after the robber, followed closely by Greg Jackson.

During the post-fight conference press, after his conquest of the UFC Light Heavyweight title, Jones described to the press what happened next:

He checked his pockets, threw on the floor his IPod, DroidX, and wallet, and asked the driver to take care of his stuff. He then began running and, because he has "*gazelle legs,*" he easily caught up with his coaches and ultimately closed on the guy they were all chasing.

Figure 1: Jackson, Jones, Winklejohn subdued a robber on March 2011

The robber was now 20 yards away.

> *"The guy looks back, and sees me, Greg and Mike. He looks back again, and the guy strips on his own foot. I start barking. The guy tries to stand up, and as he stands up, I scoops one of his ankles. He is down on the floor. I am looking at him. And then, Greg Jackson arrives and jumps on to him. I grabs his leg. The guy screams. Greg Jackson speaks to the guy in Spanish."*

And, as Mike Goldberg would conclude the story telling:

And it's all over. Just like that!

Interviewed a few hours later the incident, at about 5 p.m. in the afternoon, by Tracy Lee, Greg Jackson explained in his own word the incident:

> *"A guy stole a bunch of stuff out of a car and went running by us. Me, Jon Jones and Winklejohn came after him. Jon Jones was ahead of me, because he is that much faster, and he puts his hand on him. The guy falls down and kind of get back up and I double legged him put him on the ground, arm-barred him, Jon Jones came up behind me and put a leg lock on him, Mike Winklejohn checks his hand for weapon, and pins him down until the police came. Jones did not get hurt at all. Jones kicks his legs."*

That evening of March 19, 2011, the UFC Light Heavyweight championship around his waist, a heroic story to share with world, Jones was on top of the world. He had just defeated a legend of the sport. The media loved him. The MMA world celebrated him, his youth, his talent, his bright future.

The celebration continued for a few more month, a few more fights.

Jones defended successfully his title in September 2011 against Quinton Jackson, in December 2011 against Lyoto Machida. Next on the list was nonetheless his former training partner, friend and mentor, and now rival: Rashad *Suga* Evans.

In the *UFC Documentary: The Real Jon Jones* released on April 18, 2012 to promote their fight, Jones discussed why people were behind him, why fans were on his side:

> "*I believe that if things are simply not true, they won't stick. And I have a very strong following. And I think it's because people see my sincerity and they see the person that I am in life and as an athlete. [...] As person, I believe I am on a decent track. I am not perfect by any means, but I am on a decent track.*"

But behind closed doors, the story was different. And the world Jones wanted his fans to believe in was soon about to crumble. As he told us in the documentary, Jones was far from perfect. And Rashad Evans knew it to well. He knew how Jones really was outside the cage.

Rashad was the first one calling Jones a "*fake,*" highlighting the conflicts between Jones's public and private identities. But, at the time, everybody rooted for the young fighter, not understanding the reasons why Rashad left his former training camp to join the newly formed Blackzilians team at of Boca Raton, Florida.

We all thought Rashad was jealous, while in fact, he was simply warning us about Jones. The *religious man* Jones wanted us to believe in was indeed not so religious, not so perfect at all.

His world and attitude he depicted in the media did embrace sufficient characteristics of perfection for outsiders to believe in. But, looking closer, Jones's life was far from it. It was only deceptions.

Perhaps, Jones believed he was invulnerable, unbreakable, too-smart and too-perfect to get caught and fell hard...

Once again, on April 21, 2012, Jones did not fall. He won the fight against Rashad Evans, successfully defended for the third time his title.

But as Jones shared in the UFC Documentary, "*if things are simply not true, they won't stick.*" And clearly, his story was about to drop onto the floor. Jones was not 100% honest with his fans and the media, repeating the same story to anyone who wanted to listen.

The storyline was too simple; too simple to be real: he was a kind, humble, and always-walking-on-the-right-path type of guy. And that his wins were the sole results of his hard labor, dedication and natural talent.

And then, in Binghamton, New York, on May 19, 2012, the beautiful storyline Jones wanted us to write on his behalf, and believe in came to an unavoidable end...

May 19, 2012. Early morning: 5 a.m.

After a long night partying, and drinking like a sailor, Jones, unable to drive safely, crashed his brand new Continental GT Bentley into an utility telephone pole; the same car the UFC bought him a couple of months earlier to celebrate his rise to the UFC title.

Following the accident, an Officer from the Broome County Sheriff was dispatched to the scene. Jones's car was planted into the pole, with heavy damages to the front. No other car was involved.

Figure 2: Jon Jones's car crash on May 2012

The deputy stepped out of his police car and immediately noticed that "*there were no skids marks at the scene. It appeared as though Jones was attempting a turn north onto Helen [Street] and miscalculated his turn,*" wrote the Officer in his report.

When the Officer began questioning Jones, the uninjured driver had "*slurred speech and glassy bloodshot eyes. He smelled of alcohol and was unsteady on his feet when asked to step out of his vehicle*" reported the arresting Officer.

The Officer then asked Jones multiple times to take a sobriety and breathalyzer tests at the scene. Jones "*politely refused.*" The Officer arrested the fighter and took him into custody. While in custody, Jones kept refusing taking a sobriety and breathalyzer tests.

Binghamton Police Department Captain John Chapman explained at the time that the tests were not conducted because Jones had no serious injuries. The fighter was however charged on Driving under the influence.

Shortly after, Jones's mom, Camille Jones, came to his rescue. She drove to the Broome County Sheriff jail and bailed him out. Later that day, Jones's manager, Malki Kawa, released a statement to the media saying,

> "*I can confirm that Jon Jones was arrested early this morning on suspicion of DUI. While the facts of this situation are still being gathered and situated, First Round Management fully supports Jon, and we are asking for fans and media to respect the privacy of Jon and his family during this time.*"

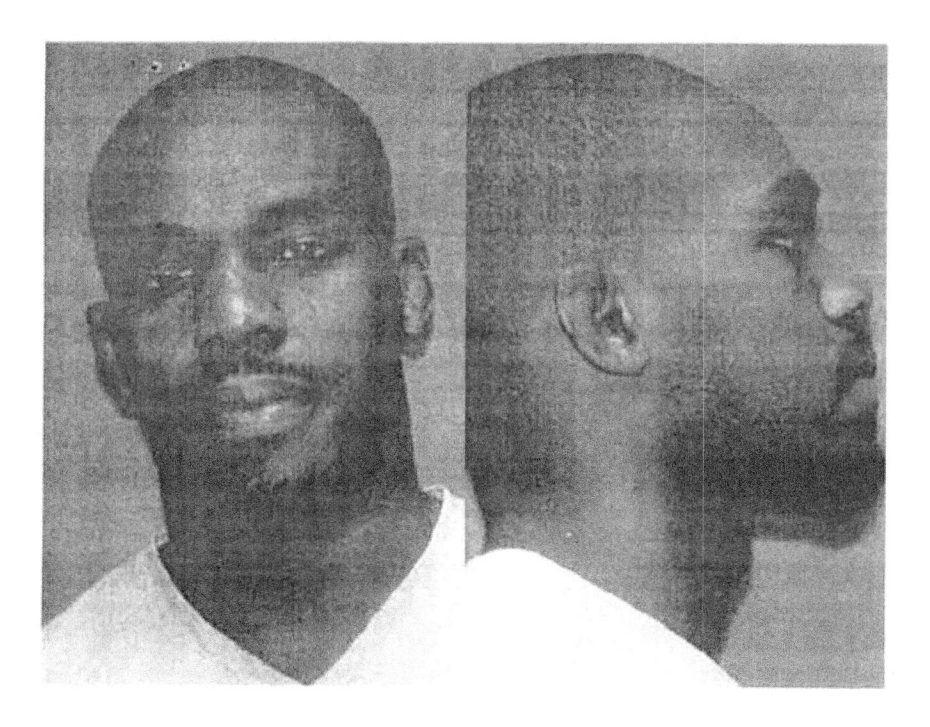

Figure 3: Jon Jones's May 2012 mugshot

"*Privacy*" was the most important word in Malki Kawa's statement. Indeed, neither his manager, nor Jones, nor the UFC wanted the reality behind the *perfect-kid* smoke screen to leak to the public. Millions were into play.

But, the truth always prevails. And, to be clear, the last 4 years of Jones's rise to fame had a lot of untold stories...

According to Sports Illustrated, the May 2012 car accident was not Jones's first car accident. He was in fact involved in several accidents in New York; one in December 2008 and another one in January 2009. For his second accident, even though his fiancée and newborn daughter were both present in the car, Jones was driving so dangerously, that he was cited for "*unsafe passing.*"

Two years later, on January 19, 2011, according to reporter Jonathan Kirschner, *Jones* was involved in another brutal collision. This time the collision was with another car whose driver, a woman, had to be carried away by paramedics on a stretcher.

Then, in November 2011, Jones was charged for driving with a suspended license and loss of traction and his car was towed away from the scene.

Based on the police report of the Albuquerque Police Department, at 3 a.m. in the morning, on November 24, 2011, Officer Dominic Martinez "*observed a black Bentley turn Northbound on Jefferson NE from Westbound McCleod NE. The vehicle came around the corner sideways and tires squealing. The vehicle continued North at a high rate of speed and pulled into the Fantasy World parking lot.*"

The *Fantasy World* is a full-nude strip club; Needless to say, for someone who had always claimed to be "*a religious guy,*" "*a Christian,*" a respectable father, and a loving fiancé, the *Fantasy World* parking lot was definitively not aligned with his faithful words, and his very-polished marketing image Jones and his closed entourage promoted since the beginning of his professional career dating from early 2008.

Officer Martinez continued and wrote in his report that he "*conducted a traffic stop and contacted the driver, identified as Jonathan Jones. I ran Jones driver's license through MVD and it was suspended. I then ran his driver's license through NCIC and they confirmed his it was suspended. Jones was cited for loss of traction and suspended driver's license. Jones vehicle was towed from the scene.*"

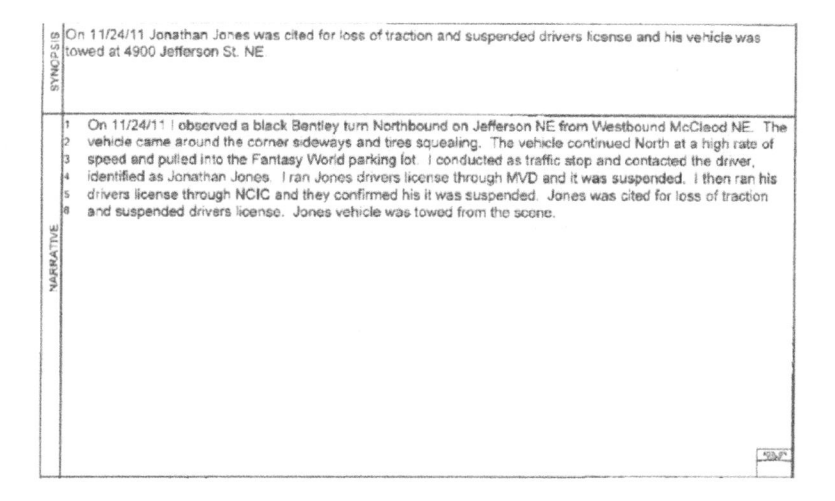

Figure 4: Officer Martinez's November 2011 Report

We should also note that at that time, Jones was still driving with a temporary license plate on his brand new 2012 Bentley. The car smelled fresh, new. Fast forward to May 2012. He crashed it onto a utility telephone pole.

Another truth Jones, his manager and the UFC did not want to release to the public was that Jones was not alone in the car at the time of the crash...

Indeed, at the time of the accident, Jones was accompanied by two young and sexy female friends: Cara Johnson, 25 years old, who was in the front passenger seat, and Michelle L. Vojtisek, 25 years old as well, sitting in the back seat. Cara Johnson was a former college basketball player at the same high-school Jones attended.

Both women suffered minor injuries. Michelle suffered bruising and cuts on the right side of her face, one above her eye and one below. Cara got a nosebleed, complained of shoulder pain, and had bruising from the seat belt. They were treated at the Wilson Hospital, and released the same day.

Figure 5: Cara Johnson and Michelle Vojtisek

Both women were obviously not Jon Jones's fiancée, Jessie Moses, with whom he already had two young daughters: Leah, born on July 11, 2008, and Carmen, born in December 2009.

We may therefore wonder why and what Jones was actually doing at 5 a.m. in the morning, after a night partying and drinking with two women other than your future wife?

I hate to jump to conclusion but, let's admit that on that early morning, Jon *Bones* Jones did not act as "*a religious guy.*" Did he forget the values his father, a Pastor, and his mother taught him and his brothers?

One would think that Jones should know better not to cheat on his fiancée, and more importantly, not to hurt his family and young daughters by behaving like a pig, a low-life dickhead, a drunk, a fake, and a fraud.

Following his arrest and release, on May 21, 2012, Jones made an apology to his friends via Facebook; an apology he soon deleted.

Reading it, we understand why he was advised to remove it from his online account...

> "*Man I haven't added anyone new to my Facebook page in like three years and right now I'm so glad that I haven't. It has literally been sickening to have so many people try to kick me while I'm down.*"

Someone should have reminded him that he was the one driving drunk at 5 a.m. in the morning after a night of party with two women other than his fiancée. But, let's not judge him. It's not our role. We just want to understand.

> "*At the same time, I totally understand, I gave them the leeway to. I screwed up, big time. Just needed to say thank you to all you guys for being amazing friends/supporters.*"

> "*Always having to deal with so many critics, haters and fickle MMA fans, I almost forgot how strong of a home base I had (607 and people that knew me before I was a champion fighter).*"

I do agree that Jones has been and is still dealing with many haters and numerous critics. As he moves on, he will face even more challenges. We can't please and appeal to everyone. But, when he was and continue being caught cheating and lying, should he expect his fans and the media to congratulate him for his constant screw-ups?

I hope not.

And, Jones's apology and explanation on Facebook ended as follows:

> *"Although the hell that will come with this hasn't even started yet, I want you guys to know how much better you've all made me feel, not only about this situation but about life, everything. It's good to feel that people are there and care. With that being said, I felt I should apologize to you first."*
>
> *"<u>I'm truly sorry to those of you that I may have embarrassed in any way, to those of you with kids that I may have let down.</u>*
>
> *I will prove to them as well as to myself that no matter what is happening in life, <u>we can always work our way back and make things even better than before.</u>*
>
> *Reading you guys uplifting comments was a great reminder for me to not give up on who I am or all the hateful people. I'm not gonna allow this situation to outweigh the positive. I love you guys right back and I promise to make things right.*
>
> *PS sorry about the terrible grammar :)"*

Clearly, two days after most likely cheating on his fiancée and mother of his daughters, Jones realized how far he was from being a religious guy, a Christian, a respectable human being, and a good father. Admitting his fault was the first step.

On May 29, 2012, Jones pleaded guilty to DWI in the Binghamton City Court. His sentence was postponed a few times but, did come later in the year; Jones was indeed fined $1,000 and his driver's license was suspended for the next six months.

The question we all wanted him to answer was however very simple: after being caught and discovered as a not-so-great person outside the cage, would he be capable of rising to the occasion and prove everyone wrong?

His next title defend was already set. He was scheduled to fight on September 1, 2012, another legend of the sport: Dan Henderson…

4   Catch and Pretend

Before answering the previous question, let's first go back in time, and dissect the statements Jones gave to the media throughout his early career, statements he made knowingly lying to (or deceiving) all...

On December 2, 2009, Jon Jones was interviewed by reporter Jack Encarnacao, UFC.com and sherdog.com. Twelve simple questions were asked about his career, upbringing and faith.

> "*Everything happens for a reason. Everything just falls into place, you know.*"

> "<u>*I've always been a person who tries to do the right thing in life*</u>, *for the most part. I'm no angel, but I* <u>*was always the kid who snitched on the kids who had pot*</u>. *I don't want to offend the pot smokers out there, but I was kind of just a snitch. I was just down for people doing the right thing. My parents kind of raised me to be a good guy. I've always been down for the good side, I guess.*"

> "*I credit my faith for pretty much everything that's been happening in my life. I'm a Pentecostal Christian (and) my dad's a pastor, so I've been going to church every Sunday since I was a small child.*"

Obviously, as we learned on May 19, 2012, the reality was very different. Luckily (I am being sarcastic here), four months later, on September 22, 2012, Jones was already a changed man, or at least he told us he was, proudly changed, adding that his DWI arrest set him free from trying to be perfect, and help him growing up as an adult.

> "*I believe in some cases MMA fans, and just fans of sports in general, have short memories. I actually believe my DUI set me free in some ways.*

It set me free from a lot of fan expectation. I was definitely coming into a sport as a young man trying to be perfect for people, and that's why people call me fake. I wasn't doing myself justice at all."

"I was kind of living miserably trying to be the golden boy for the UFC. So my DUI, it was terrible to get behind the wheel of a car while I was already under the influence, it was a bad decision, but it set me free. Now people know, yeah, I will drink on occasion, and I am a 25-year-old guy who does dumb stuff."

"I guess the biggest thing I learned from the situation is how things could have gone wrong. I could have hurt someone; I could not be sitting here right now. I could be dead and I'm blessed that didn't end up happening. My life, I'm doing so well at a lot of things and you can find yourself becoming bored in a way. Bored with such a routine in life and everything."

"So to go through such struggle and have so many people criticizing me [...] it's all a blessing. It's another opportunity to grow as a man."

But did he really grow as a man? Or was he only pretending?

Throughout his professional career, Jones had clearly inspired both admiration and hate. We all have our personal or professional opinion on him, as a fighter and a human being; his behavior inside and outside the cage does that to us. We either understands, emphasizes or we don't.

On one hand, people admire his rise to the UFC Light Heavyweight title and his impressive fighting skills.

On the other hand, people hate him for his lack of honesty and sportsmanship with his numerous *accidental* eye-gauging incidents for which he has been heavily and rightfully criticized. But, the guy who have "*always been a person who tries to do the right thing in life*", eye-gauging is a technique that on August 11, 2014, he considered normal, part of the sport, not dirty in anyway. He explained:

> "*I realize that I do it. I realize the criticism that I got from it. It's not on purpose. If you watch my fights, a lot of the times when guys get poked in the eyes, it's me extending my arm in a reactionary way. I do put a hand on people's foreheads to maintain distance. That's what you saw in the Teixeira fight, but to say I am purposely poking people in the eye, it's just inaccurate. You can call it what you want.*"

> "*I don't believe it's dirty. It's something that I do instinctually, it's something that I need to work on. It's just something that happens.*"

Many (fans, fighters and members of the press) wholeheartedly disagreed. MMA pioneer Bas Rutten, who did compete in bare-knuckled fights, even called Jon Jones a "*dirty fighter*" after his bout against Glover Teixeira.

Let's therefore remind the instinctual Jon Jones what happened to Gerard Gourdeau's opponent on April 20, 1995: Yuki Naka became permanently blind in his right eye after Gourdeau "*instinctually*" eye-gauged him.

Even Quinton *Rampage* Jackson commented on the AXS TV's "*Inside MMA*" that "*Jon Jones is bad for the sport. Because when he fights people, he injures us. He kicked my knee backwards; my knee is never the same. He's done it to a couple other guys. I saw him rip one guy's shoulder out his socket. We just try to the same thing he's trying to do, earn a living and do the sport that we love.*"

But, "*we don't go in there to try and injure people, even though I tried to fold an opponent in half, but he made me angry, it was something that he did to me…. But this guy's doing it to every opponent. He's kicking their knees backwards and really trying to hurt people. So I think that's bad for the sport."*

Enough said!

Moving on to the UFC 151!

*

Jon Jones was set to face Dan Henderson on September 1, 2012 at UFC 151. However, when Hendo injured himself and had to pull out of the fight, the UFC champion did what we all did not expected him to do, causing the cancellation of UFC 151. Little did we knew, UFC 151 was the premise of a tsunami on Jones's career.

Following his victory against Rashad Evans, *Bones* agreed to step into the octagon on September 1, 2012, at UFC 151, to face former UFC and Pride champion Dan Henderson. Unfortunately, a couple of weeks before the bout, Henderson sustained a partial rupture of his MCL and had no choice but to withdraw from the fight.

Thus, on August 23, Jones had no opponent. But, as many other fighters did and will continue doing, someone stepped up and agreed to replace the injured legend of the sport on eight days' notice. This someone was nonetheless Chael Sonnen. Chael had just lost his second bout against Anderson Silva to capture the UFC Middleweight Championship belt, but was ready to save the event and fight a larger opponent.

However, even though *Bones* once tweeted that he would never back down or refuse a fight, on that day, he did.

Figure 6: Jon Jones's May 2010 Tweet

UFC President Dana White subsequently announced that UFC 151 would be the first event in the organization's history to be cancelled.

Jones would end fighting Chael Sonnel six months later, on April 27, 2013, at UFC 159, winning by TKO. But, his reputation as a fighter had been drastically damaged. And even though, he tried to market himself as a changed and respectable man, a good guy, it was too late. And Jones certainly realized it when people began rooting for Alexander Gustafsson…

5 Talk and Feud

Following the cancellation of UFC 151, Jon *Bones* Jones returned to action to face Victor Belfort. Jones won the fight by submission, successfully defending his belt for the fourth time. He went on to fight and win Chael Sonnel at UFC 159. He was then then matched to Alexander Gustafsson.

Gustafsson was on a 5-winning streak and was bringing a new challenge to Jones; both had the same height and reach, and many wondered how Jones would adjust his traditional game plan.

The two were set to meet at UFC 165.

In the end, once again, the bout ended with Jones retaining his title. And because of back-and-forth actions, the fight was awarded the 2013 Fight of the Year by several media outlets, including MMAjunkie.com, MMAWeekly.com, Yahoo! Sports, Fox Sports, MMAfighting.com or Sherdog.com. People felt and hoped Alexander Gustafsson would be getting an immediate rematch. But, Jones refused, declining *The Viking* his well-deserved rematch.

Instead, Jones decided to fight Brazilian MMA fight Glover Texeira who was certainly a dangerous opponent but, did not bring to the cage the same level of challenge, the same level of competitiveness as Gustafsson.

Jones won the fight against Glover by unanimous decision. Jones was then matched once again to Alexander Gustafsson, who had just won his fight against with two bonuses, bringing home the Performance of the Night and Fight of the Night bonuses...

The two were to fight again at UFC 178.

Unfortunately, the rematch did not materialize. Gustafsson indeed had to pull out of the bout due to a torn right meniscus and lateral collateral ligament. And to keep the event moving forward, former Olympian and undefeated MMA fighter Daniel Cormier agreed to step in as a late replacement.

Needless to say, the promotion of this fight was a success!

Both fighters hated each other; Daniel Cormier seeing Jones as the person he really was. And this hatred translated in their now infamous brawl, where both fighters had to be physically restrained by event organizers.

On September 23, 2014, Jones who began the altercation, head-pushing his opponent during their stand-off, was given a $50,000 fine and 40 hours of community service in Las Vegas by the Nevada Athletic Commission. During the hearing Jones did what he knew best: he talked and lied...

Indeed, during the hearing, Jones claimed that because of the brawl with the former Olympian, he had lost a six-figure endorsement deal with Nike, and that this loss was "*punishment enough.*" However, that same year, Jones admitted he lied and fabricated the statement, thus committing perjury... A perjury he was never fined for!

UFC 178 ended up with not much. Jones indeed had to pull out of the fight against Daniel Cormier citing a leg injury. The two faced a few month later, on January 3, 2015 at UFC 182. *Jones* won but, as we now know, his win did not last long...

Even though he promised whoever wanted to listen to his story, Jones was still the same man, was still sailing in troubled waters.

6 Reveal and Cry

After having crashed his brand new Bentley car against a utility telephone pole in the eve of May 19, 2012, Jon Jones had clearly issues bringing consensus in the MMA community. The fans and media were either on his side or against him. No one was neutral. It was black or white.

But, when he demonstrated his superiority inside the cage and defeated Daniel Cormier (who, by the way, I was personally rooting for), the haters began rallying and standing beside Jones, while supporting the emotional Daniel Cormier in his first professional loss.

During the UFC 182 post-fight conference press, Daniel Cormier gave Jones all the credits on winning the fight, and analyzed with objectivity and calm clarity his own performance. Jones also admitted respecting his opponent.

The feud between the two fighters seemed defused, and over.

A new chapter was to begin, and Jones knew exactly what he had to do: "*All I've got to do is stay focused and keep believing, the way I believe, and then keep working. I do believe 2015 will be the year I solidify it.*"

But, the chapter Jones hoped the media would be writing on his legacy, his talent, and his genius that enable him to "*subconsciously inherit*" the talent and gifts of his opponents, did not start well...

6.1 Positive on Cocaine

On January 2015, when the news broke that Jon Jones tested positive for cocaine metabolites in an out-of-competition drug test conducted by the Nevada Athletic Commission, the champion who was "*kind of just a snitch,*" a kid who has "*always been down for the good side,*" knew he was caught - again – and in even bigger trouble than before...

The New Year was beginning on the wrong foot; 2015 was going to be a tough one for the fighter.

On December 4, 2014, 30 days before his scheduled bout at UFC 182, Jon Jones was tested by the Nevada Athletic Commission. The test result was strangely made available only right after his fight; the result: Jones tested positive for metabolites of cocaine. Cocaine!

Because cocaine is not a banned substance out of competition, the Nevada Athletic Commission allowed him to fight...

Strange world is the MMA world.

Soon after the test results were made public, Jon *The-Genius-Marketer* Jones released a statement to Yahoo Sports through his attorney acknowledging his problem:

> *"With the support of my family, I have entered into a drug treatment facility.*
>
> *I want to apologize to my fiancée, my children, as well as my mother, father, and brothers for the mistake that I made. I also want to apologize to the UFC, my coaches, my sponsors and equally important to my fans.*
>
> *I am taking this treatment program very seriously.*
>
> *Therefore, at this time my family and I would appreciate privacy."*

Great speech, right?

The UFC decided to fine the fighter $25,000 for the positive cocaine test since Jon Jones violated its athlete code of conduct. $25,000, a drop in the ocean, knowing Jones earned a disclosed payout of $500,000, not counting sponsor money, his $50,000 bonus award, and his shares on the 800,000 pay-per-view buys.

On January 18, 2015, Jones finally broke his imposed silence, explaining that "*I'm not here to make excuses. I did it. [...] I'm not gonna blame my friends. I'm not gonna blame pressure or stress. I'm not gonna blame anything ... but what I will say is that I messed up.*"

Asked how many times he used cocaine, he explained that "*cocaine is not my thing,*" adding that "*it's never been an issue,*" that "*he has his share of partying,*" and re-assuring again that he was not a cocaine addict, and that was out of his character...

But, the next day, less than 24 hours after entering rehab, after talking to several doctors, Jones checked himself out of the facility. According to the fighter, he did not need an inpatient treatment...

> "*This whole situation has been really embarrassing. I had to explain to so many people that I'm not a cocaine addict by any means or not even a frequent user. I just made a really dumb decision and got caught with my pants down in this whole situation. No excuse for it. I can just apologize.*"

But, the truth surfaced few weeks later. On November 17, 2015, Jon *Pipe* Jones admitted he had a drug problem. He was drinking, smoking frequently, he "*totally had a drug problem.*"

The consequences of his positive test for cocaine were abnormally minimal. But, his next encounter with the law would not be. His next encounter was going to squash his personal and professional world.

6.2 Hit-and-Run Charges

Four months after being caught using cocaine, on April 26, 2015, a little bit before noon, Jones's professional career took the deepest dive the fighter ever had to deal with.

And, as always, the dive began with a night of partying: girls, marijuana and alcohol.

Officers J. Brionez and Tommy Benavidez were dispatched to a traffic accident with injuries at the intersection of Juan Tabo and Southern, Albuquerque, New Mexico. The call the Police dispatch received, stated that there were three vehicles involved, with possible air bag deployment. A silver Buick SVU, a tan Toyota Camry and a maroon Honda were the vehicles reported to be involved. Callers advised that a male driver fled the scene, running north bound on Juan Tabo. The runner wore a long sleeve button down shirt.

When Officer J. Brionez arrived on scene, and advised one of the victims, Vanessa Sonnenberg. The 30-year-old woman was pregnant and complained of wrist injuries. The Officer then requested a tow truck to be brought in to take care of removing the damaged vehicles.

Officer Tommy Benavidez arrived next and observed that the three vehicles were disabled. He made contact with two drivers who refused transport by rescue. The third driver was nowhere to find. Officer Tommy Benavidez asked Vanessa Sonnenberg if she needed assistance. The victim informed him that she was pregnant, and felt like passing out. Her husband was on its way to take her to the hospital.

Interviewing the drivers, Officer Tommy Benavidez began understanding the situation. Driving her maroon Honda, Vanessa Sonnenberg was heading east on Southern, crossing through Juan Tabo, on a green light. Falsen Cambre, who was driving the tan Toyota Camry, was stopped at the red light, facing north on Juan Tabo at Southern. Falsen observed the Honda attempting to go through the greenlight when suddenly, a third vehicle, the silver Buick, turned directly into the Honda, crashing into the driver's side, pushing the Honda onto his own car. The silver Buick came to a stop.

Discussing with Bruce Benson who witnessed the accident, Officer Tommy Benavidez got more information.

Right after the crash, Bruce Benson walked toward the driver of the silver Buick, worrying about the driver's health. When Bruce asked if he was okay, the driver ignored him. The driver was busy retrieving cash from the vehicle, shoving it into his pickets.

The driver then exited his car, and fled the area by foot, running past Bruce, north into the nearby gated community.

Officer Tommy Benavidez drew the following diagram depicting the incident, where vehicle 1 is Vanessa's maroon Honda, vehicle 2 is Falsen Cambre's tan Toyota, and vehicle 3 the silver Buick.

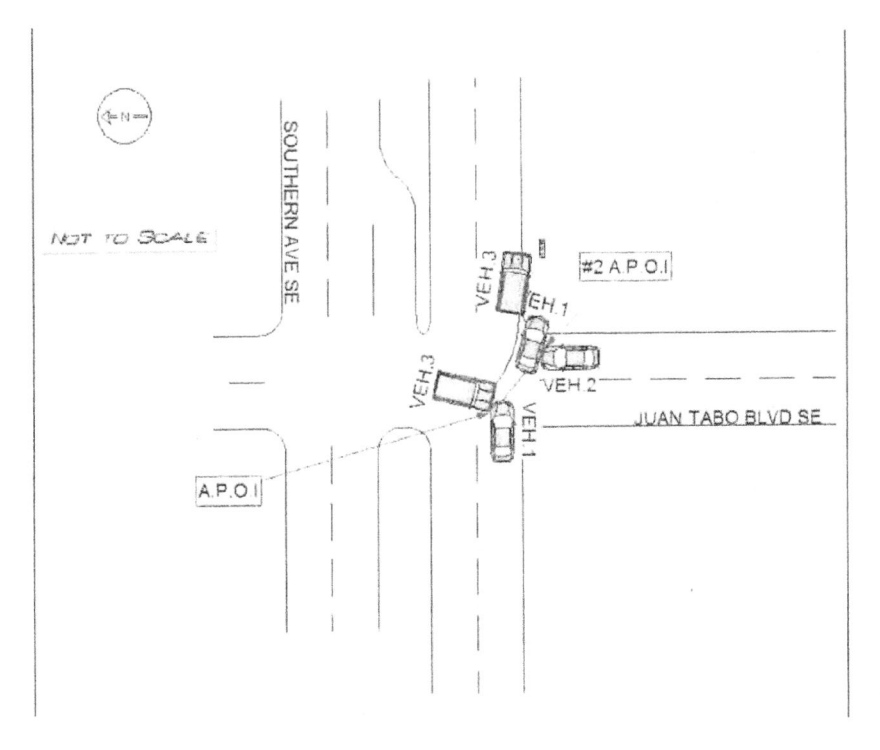

Figure 7: Jon Jones's April 2015 Hit-and-Run Accident Diagram

Driving east on Southern approaching Juan Tabo, Deputy K. Woods was off duty at the time of accident. Deputy Woods observed the multiple-car crash and stopped to check on injuries. He first blocked traffic to protect the scene, and then went on to check on Vanessa Sonnenberg.

Another off-duty Officer, Officer J. Sullivan, contacted Officer Tommy Benavidez. He was indeed driving on Southern from Juan Tabo, and was at the traffic accident scene right after. He noticed the driver of silver Buick and immediately recognized him: "*Jon Jones was wearing a nice white polo style short, with either dark jeans or slacks on.*"

Officer J. Sullivan observed the MMA fighter jogging in front of the vehicle and going up to the hill on the south east corner of Juan Tabo and Southern. After a few minutes, Jon Jones ran back to the silver Buick, entered the vehicle from the driver's door, and fled the scene again.

In addition to the two witnesses who identified Jon Jones, Officer J. Brionez conducted a search incident to tow the Buick and found compromising evidences against Jon Jones: a marijuana pipe with marijuana inside it, paperwork belonging to the MMA fighter, including a phone number.

Officer Tommy Benavidez called several times the phone number belonging to Jon Jones, leaving two voicemails, and recommending the fighter to call 911 immediately. Jones never called back.

In the meantime, Vanessa Sonnenberg had been treated at the Kaseman hospital where she learned she had a fractured arm and wrist.

Her baby seemed to be okay.

And so, following the interviews, the evidences discovered in the rental car, and not having heard back from Jon Jones or his attorneys, the County of Bernalillo decided to proceed forward and requested an arrest warrant be issued for Jon Jones on violation of sections 66-7-201c: Accidents involving death or personal injuries.

ROAD	VEH NO.	Road Condition	Road Surface	Traffic Control	Road Lanes	Road Design Div	Road Design
	03	DRY	PAVED CENTER AND EDGE LIN	TRAFFIC SIGNALS	2 LANES	PAINTED DIVIDE	FULL ACCESS CT

	APPARENT CONTRIBUTING FACTORS	DRIVER'S ACTIONS	SEQUENCE OF EVENTS	
EVENT	AVOID NO CONTACT - OTHER, AVOID NO CONTACT VEHICLE, DISREGARDED TRAFFIC SIGNAL, DRIVER INATTENTION, EXCESSIVE SPEED, MADE IMPROPER TURN, OTHER IMPROPER DRIVING, UNDER INFLUENCE OF DRUGS OR MEDICATION	LEFT TURN	FIRST EVENT	MVT
			SECOND EVENT	MVT
			THIRD EVENT	MVT
			FOURTH EVENT	MVT

DRIVER	DRIVER/PEDESTRIAN/PEDALCYCLIST SOBRIETY	DRIVER/PED/PEDAL CYCLIST PHYSICAL CONDITION	PEDESTRIAN	PEDESTRIAN/PEDALCYCLIST ACTION
	SOBRIETY UNKNOWN	NO APP. DEFECTS		At Intersection
				Not At Intersection
	Breath Test Results	Driver Physical Condition - Other		Pedestrian Action - Other

NARRATIVE

ON 04/26/2015, OFC. J. BRIONEZ AND I WERE DISPATCHED TO A HIT AND RUN TRAFFIC ACCIDENT, AT THE INTERSECTION OF JUAN TABO AND SOUTHERN. CALLER STATED THE DRIVER OF A SILVER SUV RAN FROM THE ACCIDENT. OFC. BRIONEZ AND I ARRIVED, WITH RESCUE ARRIVING ON SCENE SHORTLY AFTER. THE DRIVER OF BOTH VEHICLES REFUSED RESCUE. THE DRIVER OF THE HONDA STATED HER HUSBAND WILL TAKE HER. DRIVER ONE STATED SHE WAS HEADING EAST IN LANE 2, AND WAS CROSSING THOUGH JUAN TABO ON A GREEN LIGHT, WHEN DRIVER 3 RAN THE LIGHT HITTING HER ON THE DRIVER SIDE. DRIVER 2 STATED HE WAS WAITING AT A RED LIGHT FACING NORTH ON JUAN TABO AT SOUTHERN. DRIVER 2 STATED WHEN DRIVER 1 WAS CROSSING ON A GREEN LIGHT, DRIVER 3 TURNED INTO HER FROM THE SOUTHBOUND TURN LANE OF SOUTHERN HITTING HER DRIVER SIDE. WITNESSES AND DRIVERS FROM BOTH VEHICLES, STATED DRIVER OF VEHICLE 3 GOT OUT AND LEFT RUNNING. WITNESSES STATED THE DRIVER OF VEHICLE 3, EXITED AFTER HITTING THE HONDA AND WAS IDENTIFIED AS A BLACK MALE, WEARING A WHITE BUTTON UP SHIRT, WITH DARK PANTS ON AND RAN ONTO A HILL JUST EAST OF THE ACCIDENT. WITNESSES STATED HE SLOUCHED OVER AND RAN BACK TO THE VEHICLE GRABBING A LARGE HAND FULL OF CASH. WITNESSES STATED THE DRIVER SHOVED THE CASH INTO HIS PANTS AND RAN NORTH JUMPING THE FENCE INTO TERRACITA. I SENT OFFICERS TO ATTEMPT TO LOCATE THE DRIVER OF VEHICLE 3. THE OFFICERS WHO ATTEMPTED TO LOOK FOR HIM, WERE UN SUCCESSFUL. DRIVER 1 WAS TAKEN TO KASEMAN HOSPITAL DUE TO BEING PREGNANT AND FEELING LIKE SHE WAS GOING TO PASS OUT. OFC. BRIONEZ AND I CONDUCTED A SEARCH INCIDENT TO TOW ON THE BUICK. OFC. BRIONEZ FOUND A MARIJUANA PIPE, WITH MARIJUANA INSIDE OF IT, AND TAGGED IT INTO EVIDENCE. I LOCATED PAPERWORK BELONGING TO A JONATHAN JONES, WHICH HAD MMA INFORMATION ON IT. I WAS ABLE TO LOCATE A PHONE NUMBER FOR JON JONES AND PLACED SEVERAL PHONE CALLS WITH NO SUCCESS. I LEFT A MESSAGE FOR JON JONES TO CALL DISPATCH, BUT NEVER RECEIVED ONE. THE PAPERWORK, WILL BE TAGGED INTO EVIDENCE.

Figure 8: Extract from the Jon Jones's Accident Police Report

STATE OF NEW MEXICO
-VS-

ARTICLE 2
INITIATION OF PROCEEDINGS
STATE OF NEW MEXICO
COUNTY OF BERNALILLO
IN THE METROPOLITAN COURT

Name: Jonathan Jones
Address: ▬▬▬▬▬
Albuquerque, NM 87111
D.O.B.: ▬▬▬▬▬
S.S.N.: unknown
Charge: Leaving the scene of an accident involving death or personal injuries.

Arrest Date:
Driver Lic. #: ▬▬▬▬▬
Citation #:
Arrest #:
Docket #:
Date Filed: 04/27/2015

Complainant or Officer: Det. T. Benavidez   Man #: 5383

CRIMINAL COMPLAINT- ARREST WARRANT AFFIDAVIT

Figure 9: Jon Jones's April 2015 Arrest Warrant

Jon Jones now had an arrest warrant floating on his head for his involvement in the accident. He was a wanted man. Ironically, three week prior becoming a wanted man, Jones had posted on Instagram about how he had "*matured*" since his 2012 car crash.

On April 26, 2015, maturity came in a very odd form: a scared fighter running away from his responsibilities...

The arrest warrant issued, the Albuquerque Police Department began searching for the fighter.

The next day, Police spokesman Simon Drobik told reporters that they still "*don't know where he is right now,*" "*we're trying to figure that out.*"

A second Police Department spokesman, Tanner Tixier, explained that if Jon ones wanted to reach out to the Police, it should not be challenging: many of Officers trained at the Jackson-Winkeljohn MMA gym...

A few hours later, the Albuquerque Police Department also announced via Twitter that arrangements were made for the fugitive to turn himself in.

Albuquerque Police
@ABQPOLICE

An arrest warrant issued for UFC fighter Jon Jones. cabq.gov/police/documen... Arrangements have been made for Mr. Jones to turn himself in

3:37 PM - 27 Apr 2015

328   102

Figure 10: Albuquerque Police's April 2015 Tweet

At 6:42 p.m. the Albuquerque Police informed via Tweeter than Jon Jones had been booked at the Bernalillo County Metropolitan Detention Center without incident.

And, at 10 p.m., after posting a $2,500 bail, Jon *Bones* Jones was already released...

Figure 11: Jon Jones's April 2015 mugshot

Following a fairly inconsequential day (booked and released in 3 hours), Jones began feeling the pressure and the immediate downside of continuously misbehaving – to say the least.

On April 28, 2017, the UFC stripped him of his Light Heavyweight title, releasing a statement clearly condemning, while supporting the fighter in its most recent encounter with the law:

"As a result of the charge and other violations of the Athlete Code of Conduct Policy, the organization believes it is best to allow Jones time to focus on his pending legal matters."

"UFC feels strongly that its athletes must uphold certain standards both in and out of the Octagon. While there is disappointment in the recent charges, the organization remains supportive of Jones as he works through the legal process."

Jones was no longer the UFC champion. The same day, most certainly sober, he took it to Tweeter, breaking his silence:

"Got a lot of soul searching to do. Sorry to everyone I've let down."

The next day, on April 29, 2015, financial consequences came to Jones. Reebok ripped apart his agreement with the athlete. The year before, it was Nike that parted away from the champion, and MMA in general. This is what happened when large brands decide to sponsor the wrong athletes. An entire sport suffered.

A week later, the Albuquerque Police released a video taken by the Officers while searching Jones's rental car after the accident. Not only the Officers found pipe, marijuana, cash, dirty clothes, water bottles and loose change, they also found a box of condoms... *Bones* had a bone.

Stripped of the UFC Light Heavyweight title, no longer endorsed by Reebok, Jon *Bones* Jones had now to face the results of his not-so-faithful and Christian behavior; he was now in trouble with his fiancée of two years, Jessie Moses, the mother of his three daughters.

The summer of 2015 went by, day by day. Jones did his best to stay away from the headlines. Daniel Cormier became the UFC Light Heavyweight Champion, submitting Anthony Johnson at UFC 187. Jon Jones and Jessie Moses stayed together; which makes me wonder if the two are actually in an open-relationship. Modern era.

And with the spring of 2015 came the sentencing. On September 29, 2015, Jones pleaded guilty to charges stemming from his hit-and-run crash, avoiding jail time, a felony conviction, fines and other restrictions traditionally imposed on parolees. Lucky guy.

Judge Charles Brown of the Second Judicial District Court ordered Jones to serve 18 months of probation (72 weeks) and make 72 appearances speaking to local youth about what he learned from his "*stupid decision.*"

> "*Mr. Jones, you got real lucky, and in a number of ways, I think you need to talk to young people because making one stupid decision changes your entire future.*"

> "*I want to apologize to Ms. Sonnenburg's team, all the Officers who were involved that day, all the people who support me that I've embarrassed, my family, mainly Vanessa Sonnenburg and her family for all the heartache that I must have put them through,*" Jones said during the hearing, adding: "*I am here to accept full responsibility for what happened, and I hope you can give me an opportunity to redeem myself.*"

Jones also released a statement through his management after the court made its ruling.

> "*With regards to today's decision made by the court, I am very happy to now be able to put this incident behind me. My actions have caused pain and inconvenience in the lives of others and for that I am truly sorry and I accept full responsibility.*

I have been working hard during this time away from my sport to grow and mature as a man and to ensure that nothing like this happens again. I have learned a great deal from this situation and I am determined to emerge a better person because of it."

"I apologize to those who were affected by my actions in this incident and I am hopeful that I will be given the opportunity to redeem myself in the eyes of the public, my family and friends as well as my supporters. I am not sure what the future holds for me but I plan to continue to do the work needed to be productive and successful in every aspect of my life."

A month later, on October 23, 2015, the UFC lifted his suspension, clearing the notorious fighter to return to action and bring pay-per-view buys to the promotion. The same day, happy-Jones told the media that he was both grateful for the opportunity and excited *"to show how much I've grown as a person outside of the octagon."*

"It took me losing almost everything I had worked for to realize how much I had. […] This marks the beginning of a new chapter in my life and my career and let me assure you the best is yet to come."

When *Bones* told the press about this new beginning, I had a flashback, and remembered UFC 182 post-fight conference press. That evening, proud of his impressive win over Daniel Cormier, Jones told the media about his plan for 2015:

"All I've got to do is stay focused and keep believing, the way I believe, and then keep working. I do believe 2015 will be the year I solidify it."

In a strangely ironic way, 2015 turned exactly how he wanted it to be.

His life outside the cage (i.e.: the partying, the alcohol, the drugs, the careless driving, and the women) solidified and cracked wide open for the world to see. In my opinion, it was only a matter of time for his constant personal mistakes to be exposed to the limelight and the consequences to spill onto his professional life.

Jones began 2015 as the undisputed UFC Light Heavyweight champion. He then lost his title and endorsements, faced the penalties of his actions, and ended the year with new resolutions for 2016…

6.3   Drag-Racing Charges

Rashad Evans was the first one calling *Bones* a "*fake,*" highlighting the conflicts between *Bones*'s public and private identities. It was back in 2012, days before Jones, under the influence, crashed his brand new Bentley on a utility telephone pole.

For the next three years, from 2012 to 2015, Jones did not change a bit. He was still a different person at work and at home.

At work, he was the Christian playing by the rules, "*the kid who snitched on the kids who had pot,*" the kind of person who did "*the right thing.*"

At home, he drank, smoked marijuana, sniffed cocaine, and partied with women other than his beautiful fiancée, the mother of his three daughters.

And so, when 2015 ended, and 2016 began, we all had two simple and straightforward questions in mind:

- Did Bones really learn from his previous ordeals and finally change for the better?
- When would he return to action? We did not know where and when, but, we all hoped his opponent would be Daniel Cormier.

Unfortunately, not one month in the New Year, on January 31, 2016, Jones once again headlined the news.

This time, no alcohol or drug was involved; an improvement. But, his driving did not improve much. He was pulled over in Albuquerque, New Mexico, speeding.

"The reason I stopped you, you're going 75 down Alameda in a 35, okay?" the Officer told Jones.

The recently pardoned UFC fighter was driving 75 miles per hour in a 35-mile-per-hour zone. But not only he was speeding, he was driving without a license, proof of registration, and proof of insurance on him; which is, needless to explain, illegal. And, when someone is on probation, even speeding opens doors to potential consequences nastier than a simple fine for a traffic violation.

If you listen to the audio released by the Albuquerque Police Department, Jon Jones did not sound under the influence. He spoke intelligently and calmly to the Officer, listening and somehow acknowledging his faults. This most likely explained why the Officer was lenient and did not to write the fighter a citation for reckless driving.

"You're getting a huge break dude," said the Officer. Jon Jones acknowledged, and he was on its way. The end... or almost.

On February 6, 2016, the UFC announced what we all were waiting for; Jones's return into the octagon. The long-awaited and anticipated rematch with Daniel Cormier was set. The two were to meet in Las Vegas, on April 23, 2016, and headlined the UFC 197 card.

We all had one thing to say: Yay! At last!

He was back!

Thus, finally, the media published the many articles reporters drafted and prepared long ago. The articles had one goal: summing up Jon Jones's professional career and adventures outside the cage. The UFC also released a first promotional spot... The *Bones* machine was once again rolling.

But, two days later, reporters adjusted the storyline to focus on Jones's potential spoiled return. Following his speeding infraction, Jones had a planned date with the Court.

As Kayla Anderson, Public Information Officer for the Second Judicial District Attorney's Office in New Mexico, explained to MMAWeekly.com, "*all defendants being supervised on probation are required generally to not violate any laws.*" And, because *Bones* did violate the law, the District Attorney "*has the discretion to pursue a revocation of probation if an alleged incident arises to the level of a substantial violation of probation.*"

Later that day, the District Attorney's office made its ruling. The DA would not look at "*filing a formal probation violation.*" Unquestionably, Jones got another big break from the law and the judicial system. And, by the same token, the anticipated money-maker UFC 197 was saved; or at least, saved for a couple of months, as we now know.

On Thursday, March 24, 2016, Jon Jones was – surprise! – pulled over.

This time, he was no longer cordial and calm.

In the video released to the public a few days later, we can hear the Officer asking why the driver, Jon Jones, was drag-racing a Cadillac.

Watching the video, you can immediately observe the first mistake Jon Jones made: when you are being pulled over, you do not laugh and argue vehemently with the officer. You may disagree and have a different view on the incident (if any) but, you keep it to yourself. Argumentation can be presented at a later time, in court, after disputing the issued traffic violation.

But, right off the bat, Jon Jones began confronting Officer Brown, and complied very slowly with the Officer's request. After Jones finally handed the Officer his registration, license and proof of insurance, Officer Brown began walking back, suggesting the fighter to "*cut the attitude.*"

When Officer Brown returned to Jones's car, he gave and explained the fighter the several traffic violations he wrote. This is when Jon Jones committed his second mistake; a big one.

After Officer Brown handed the written violations, asking if Jon Jones understood and acknowledged the court date. But instead of simply signing the paperwork, Jones decided to go on record, and then, lost his temper, ending by "*You are an absolute f–king liar,*" and "*I can't wait until you get out of my face. You're despicable. Pig. You disgust me.*"

Figure 12: Jon Jones's March 24 2016 Police Camera Cam

Five days later, on Tuesday March 29, 2016, Jon *Bones* Jones had no choice but to surrender to the police. A judge had issued an arrest warrant for his arrest after learning the fighter was cited for five new traffic violations, including drag racing, exhibition driving and weaving.

He was arrested by his Probation Officer, and placed into custody, pending the preparation and review of his probation violation report by the Bernalillo County District Attorney.

Figure 13: Jon Jones's March 24 2016 Booking Information

In custody, the media began imagining the cancellation of his upcoming fight against Daniel Cormier.

It was the end of March 2016, and in less than a month, on April 23 at UFC 197, the two were set to face one more time and fight for the undisputed Light Heavyweight Championship Title.

But, this time, both fighters had traded places; DC had now the belt, and *Bones* was the challenger. Needless to say, with one fighter in jail, the UFC 197 main event was in danger of being cancelled.

Figure 14: Jon Jones's March 2016 mugshot

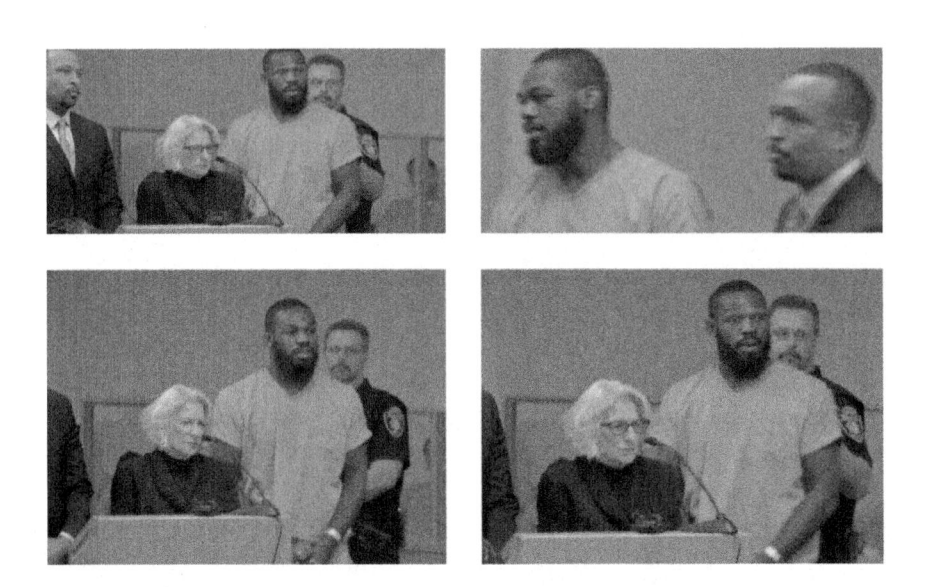

Figure 15: Jon Jones's March 2016 arraignment

Two days after his incarceration, Jones agreed to a plea deal. He was then released. Once more (recurring story), the plea deal allowed the fighter to avoid jail time; when you can pay the right lawyers, justice tends to be forgiving.

According to MMAFighting.com, Jon *Bones* Jones was released on March 31, 2016 and ordered to complete 60 hours of community service, as well as courses in driver improvement and anger management.

Jones avoiding major consequences from his constant dangerous driving, the UFC had to do something, to follow the rules of its Athlete Code of Conduct. And, so, the UFC issued a harsh statement (yes, I am being sarcastic): they were "*disappointed.*"

> "*UFC respects the decision made today by Judge Michael E. Martinez in New Mexico Second Judicial District Court regarding the probation terms of the case involving Jon Jones.*"

> "*The organization was disappointed to learn that Jones was cited for several traffic offenses last week, as well as concerned by the nature and tone of portions of the conversation between Jones and the citing officer.*"

> "*Still, UFC respects Jones' right to contest those traffic citations in court and receive a fair hearing on the matter.*"

> "*Jones' scheduled bout on April 23 will proceed as planned, however, Jones understands that the UFC expects him to fully cooperate with the terms of his probation as set forth by Judge Martinez.*"

Long story short, the UFC had no intention, no will, and no interest in changing its plan for the upcoming UFC 197; too much money had already been sunk into the promotion and organization of event.

But, on April 1st, the plan ultimately changed: Daniel Cormier pulled out of the fight after injuring his foot in training. Ovince Saint Preux was asked to step-up and replace DC. The rest belongs to the MMA history.

Following his successful return into the octagon, Jones explained to the world that the car crash on April 2015 was a blessing in the sky, that he learned his lessons:

> *"It was a reality check. That's really what it all boils down to for me. It was the day that I realized that life wasn't all fun and games, there are consequences for your actions."*

> *"I've told my story 72 times to completely different groups, to complete strangers. There's something really freeing about being so real, open and candid with complete strangers and letting them judge you."*

He was a changed man.

> *"I got a lot of proving to do. It's a matter of actions. It's about my effort. I feel like I have a lot more work to do. The people who still hate me, they have every right to."*

Knowing how 2016 ended for the fighter, re-reading his statements, I can't stop thinking that he purposely leveraged the 72 court-ordered public speaking appearances as dress-rehearsals; preparing his comeback speech, ensuring all was perfect: word, tone, pause, tears, everything. Looking back, I truly believe it was just another sham, another con.

Regardless, on April 23, 2016, Jones made a successful return, winning the fight against Ovince (in a very unimpressive fashion). And since the UFC wanted to reward the recidivist, Jones was crowned the Interim Light Heavyweight Champion.

Days later, rumors began to surface about his next bout: DC at UFC 200...

6.4 Anti-Doping Policy Violation

When the UFC began planning the infamous UFC 200, everyone wanted to know what was coming up; where, when, and who. The UFC only had one word to the media: Wait.

Wait until they tell us what to write. The UFC was on the verge of being sold and rumors were spreading all around. Thus, for UFC 200, the UFC executives wanted to muzzle the press. And, of course, as always should I say, it did not go as planned. Why? Because the UFC had forgotten one basic concept: we are free to report on what we know.

Conor McGregor and Nate Diaz were to headline the card. But, when the Irish fighter refused to show up at a scheduled conference press, the UFC switched stand and, on April 27, 2017, the UFC announced Daniel Cormier vs. Jon Jones as the new headliner.

And, then, rumors surfaced and became facts: Brock Lesnar was to return. Ariel Helwani, E. Casey Laydon, and Esther Lin informed the fans about the news before the UFC official announcement... We then observed the worst dick move in MMA: the UFC revoked their credentials, escorted them out of The Forum where UFC 199 was held, and decided to ban the journalists for life; a ban that would be removed a few days later thanks to the pressure of free press. All of that to simply say that UFC 200 was not – and by far – the best organized event of the giant MMA promotion.

As we all expected, the feud between DC and *Bones* was still very present in the air. On July 6, 2016, at 3 p.m. Eastern Time, the pre-conference press stand-off between the two were intense. We were all in for a good brawl, a fight to remember.

A fight that was not meant to be...

A few hours later, the UFC called in emergency another conference press. On stage, Dana White and Daniel Cormier. Dana White's first words during this press conference: "*The main event is Mark Hunt vs. Brock Lesnar.*"

Jon Jones had indeed been pulled out from his scheduled fight by the United States Anti-Doping Agency (USADA) due to a potential Anti-Doping Policy violation stemming from an out-of-competition sample collection on June 16, 2016.

Learning the news at 7:53 p.m. Central Time that Jones had cheated and got caught for violating the USADA policy, DC was naturally pissed but he was still ready to fight, asks if he could sign a release form and enable the fight to proceed forward. "*I can't do it,*" replied UFC President Dana White.

That evening, we observed DC, genuinely devastated, and more than that, candidly sad. He was sincerely sad. Sad for having trained so hard to prove to the world that he would have squashed the *new, improved and changed* Jon Jones. Sad for not being compensated for all his hard and honest work in the gym. Sad for Jon Jones's family and friends to have to deal with one more screw-up of their fiancé, father, brother, child and friend.

A day later, Jon *Bones* Jones apologized for this violation but, as he always did (even when he is the one driving the car), he vehemently denied any wrongdoings, denied taking any illegal substances. And he even spilled a few (crocodile) tears.

Then, on July 22, 2016, the USADA informed him that the potential sanction was one year period of ineligibility, beginning on July 6, 2016. And, as many other stories involving Jon Jones, lawyers had to be called to get him out of troubled waters. Their objective: fight against the USADA and do their best to avoid or reduce the duration of Jones's suspension. Millions of dollars were at stake.

On or about July 25, 2016, *Jones's* attorney sent a few items to test to the Korva laboratories:

1. A sealed silver pouch of Tadalafil of the kind said to have been ingested by the fighter,

2. A bottle of T-Anabol, a WADC compliant product that he had been taking since 2011.

Tests were conducted in August 2016.

The Tadalafil tests showed positive for clomiphene and letrozole, the same substances found in Jones's samples. The source of Jones's positive test was now known. The only question people wanted to understand was simple: how did the fighter took this drug?

After training with MMA fighter and teammate Eric Blasich, on or about June 14, 2016, while both men were out dinning, Eric told Jones that he had been using a product called Cialis; a product Jones understood as a product like Viagra, which he had previously used. As the conversation continued, Eric gave *Bones* the "*dick pill.*"

The next question you may ask: Why?

Why did a more than healthy 29 years old man, in the prime of his age, would take a capsule helping erectile dysfunction?

Unfortunately, only Jones *Cartilage* Jones knows the why he took this pill.

We are therefore left with hypothesis: was Jones planning to attend one of his traditional pre-fight parties? The type of parties he used to go to a week prior to his fights, party always involving alcohol, drugs, and women. The timing of the incident seemed about right. You tell me.

On November 6, 2016, the USDA Panel directed by Michael J. Belloff, and arbitrated by Lars Halgreen and Markus Manninen handed the fighter a 12-month suspension, beginning on July 6, 2016:

> 13.1. The Panel repeats that the Applicant's fault was at the top end of the scale. In short, the Applicant made an advance enquiry about a product Cialis which he did not take. He made no enquiry at all about the Tadalafil pill which he did take. He simply relied

upon his team mate to tell him what it was and how it could enhance sexual pleasure. His degree of fault in fact verged on the reckless. It therefore concludes that the maximum sanction of twelve months subject only to the deduction of the period of suspension served will be consonant with the facts as found. It notes that the maximum penalty for specified substances is half that required by the WADC and cannot be said to infringe any principle of proportionality.

14. . EPILOGUE

On the evidence before the Panel, the Applicant is not a drug cheat. He did not know that the tablet he took contained prohibited substances or that those substances had the capacity to enhance sporting performance. However by his imprudent use of what he pungently referred to as a "*dick pill*" he has not only lost a year of his career but an estimated nine million dollars. This outcome which he admits to be a wake-up call for him should serve as a warning to all others who participate in the same sport.

7   Talk and...

Jones finally came completely clean in December 2016. Interviews by several outlets, the suspended fighter told his *behind the scenes* story.

> *"I had this crazy thing that I would do where I would party one week before every fight and I did that throughout my whole career. It was stupid, but it was this mental crutch that I had. I literally would one week before every fight, I would go out, I would get blacked out wasted."*

> *"My logic was if this guy was to beat me somehow I can look myself in the mirror and say that I lost because I got hammered the week before the fight. It was a safety net. I did it my whole career. I would go out and get hammered one week before every fight."*

His constant partying almost costed him the fight of year against Alexander Gustafsson at UFC 165, on September 21, 2013.

> *"I had this feeling that I was invincible and I did a lot of wild stuff leading up to that fight. I definitely didn't give it my all. Mainly partying, drinking, and staying up all night."*

> *"I just felt in no way, shape, or form did he have what it took to beat me. Sure enough, after round two, I was pretty gassed out. That was the first time in my whole career being tired in the second round. It just went to show that my cardio, my focus, everything, it just wasn't there."*

> *"I partied my tail off for Gustafsson, I almost lose but obviously still win the fight, and I won the fight knowing that I didn't deserve to win that fight. That really was what lead me to not taking*

> anything seriously. [...] I really developed the attitude of, 'I can have fun and still do my job.'"

And, then came April 2015 and the hit-and-run.

> "I stopped answering my phone calls for a lot of people and I just went into hiding for a while. I just stayed away from the scene until I felt like I was strong enough not to do it. It helped a lot."

> "I'm honestly excited to be set free from that. It took me a long time to acknowledge that I had a little bit of a problem because I was able to take care of my family. I was able to win fights. I was able to pretty much hide it from the world, that I was smoking pot and drinking three or four days a week. I was handling my life so I didn't think I had a problem."

> "But now that I'm completely sober, I totally had a problem."

> "My life has changed for the better in so many different ways since this car accident. I'm grateful for it."

Since his removal from UFC 200, Jon *Bones* Jones has been heard apologizing and recognizing the many mistakes he did in the past.

He has made amends.

As MMA fans, we now have three options.

1. The first one would be to consider the multiple relapses Jones has had in the past, telling us he is changed man, and a few weeks or months later, being caught his pants down again.

2. The second option would be to believe in his most recent change, placing our confidence, trust and support in the new Jon Bones Jones, and looking forward to seeing him soon competing inside the octagon.

3. The third one would be to give him a chance in demonstrating that this time, he has indeed changed for the better, and wishing him all the very best in his next adventures, inside or outside the cage.

Personally, I feel that Jon *Bones* Jones deserved another shot at earning the support of MMA fans. If his next fight happened to be a pay-per-view, I will not purchase it, but, perhaps, I will spend the money for his second bout. Only time will tell.

Sadly, for now, the story ends here, with a *To Be Continued*...

Jon Jones, we look forward to seeing you sober, healthy and truly happy. Life, God, gave you amazing gifts. Use them right. Use them to support and provide your family, your loved ones, and your daughters. Use them to prove that our sport is for people who wants to improve themselves, who wants to do better, inside and outside the cage.

This page left blank intentionally

For More Information

References

The information presented in this mini book is gathered from various online sources. If you would to know more about the crimes committed by these MMA fighters, feel free to refer to the following links:

Section	URL
1	https://en.wikipedia.org/wiki/Jon_Jones
1	http://prommanow.com/2012/04/18/ufc-documentary-the-real-jon-jones/
1	http://www.fighthype.com/pages/content3394.html
1	http://www.mmafighting.com/ufc/2012/4/20/2960094/morning-report-from-amateur-to-ufc-145-in-three-months-a-jon-jones-video-timeline-mma
1	https://www.youtube.com/watch?v=cpPoXfh8ZuI
3	http://bleacherreport.com/articles/1189805-jon-jones-dwi-real-photo-of-ufc-champs-wrecked-bentley-surfaces
3	http://sports.yahoo.com/mma/blog/cagewriter/post/hours-before-biggest-fight-of-his-life-jones-and-trainers-catch-a-robber-in-new-jersey?urn=mma,wp309
3	http://sports.yahoo.com/news/jon-jones-dwi-arrest-set-012456052--mma.html
3	http://www.bjpenn.com/mmanews/police-report-evidences-jon-jones-had-prior-legal-issues-ufc-news/
3	http://www.bloodyelbow.com/2012/5/21/3034531/police-report-jon-jones-ufc-drivers-license-dui
3	http://www.cagepotato.com/breaking-jon-jones-arrested-for-dui-in-binghamton-ny/
3	http://www.fightersonlymag.com/content/news/17129-dana-qwe-bought-jones-a-bentley
3	http://www.mmamania.com/2012/5/20/3033193/jon-jones-car-crash-pic-video-Binghamton-NY-UFC
3	http://www.mmamania.com/2012/5/21/3034258/jon-jones-facebook-apology-twitter-bones-ufc-151-dan-henderson
3	http://www.mmamania.com/2012/5/29/3050013/ufc-jon-jones-pleads-guilty-dwi-sentencing-june-19-binghamton
3	http://www.mmamania.com/2012/5/30/3053930/pic-jon-jones-female-passenger-cara-johnson-who-was-in-the-car-that
3	http://www.si.com/more-sports/2012/05/30/jones

Section	URL
3	http://www.tmz.com/2012/05/19/jon-jones-ufc-arrested-dui/
3	https://www.scribd.com/doc/94333552/Jonathon-Jones
4	http://bleacherreport.com/articles/2158980-jon-jones-on-eye-pokes-i-dont-believe-its-dirty
4	http://sports.yahoo.com/news/jon-jones-dwi-arrest-set-012456052--mma.html
4	http://www.sherdog.com/news/articles/1/12-Questions-for-Jon-Jones-21220
4	http://www.sherdog.com/news/news/Rampage-Jackson-Says-Jon-Jones-Is-Bad-for-the-Sport-Because-He-Injures-Opponents-94571
4	https://en.wikipedia.org/wiki/UFC_151
5	http://www.bloodyelbow.com/2014/12/29/7465221/mma-news-jon-jones-admits-he-lied-about-ufc-brawl-with-cormier-nike-deal-loss
5	http://www.fightersonlymag.com/content/news/17129-dana-qwe-bought-jones-a-bentley
5	http://www.mmamania.com/2014/9/23/6833967/jon-jones-dumped-by-nike-lost-six-figure-endorsement-deal-daniel-cormier-media-brawl-mma
6	http://ftw.usatoday.com/2015/01/ufc-star-jon-jones-cocaine-test-interview
6	http://heavy.com/news/2015/04/jon-jones-hit-and-run-suspect-sought-for-questioning-ufc-187-charges-arrest-albuquerque-new-mexico-police-victim-car-crash-accident-rumor/
6	http://hollywoodlife.com/2016/03/28/jon-jones-yelling-police-officer-traffic-stop-video/
6	http://hollywoodlife.com/2016/07/07/jon-jones-removed-from-ufc-200-daniel-cormier-fails-drug-test-doping/
6	http://mmajunkie.com/2015/04/witnesses-jon-jones-fled-hit-and-run-scene-with-handful-of-cash-pot-found-in-rental-car
6	http://mmajunkie.com/2016/03/ufc-disappointed-with-jon-jones-but-ufc-197-headliner-is-still-a-go
6	http://nypost.com/2015/04/27/cops-want-ufc-star-jon-jones-after-pregnant-lady-hurt-in-hit-and-run/
6	http://www.cnn.com/2015/04/29/us/ufc-jon-bones-jones-hit-and-run/
6	http://www.forbes.com/sites/mattconnolly/2016/03/29/jon-jones-arrested-for-violating-probation-timeline-of-ufc-stars-transgressions-and-whats-next/#1c4294ac1bd3
6	http://www.foxsports.com/ufc/story/jon-jones-i-totally-had-a-drug-problem-112715

Section	URL
6	http://www.foxsports.com/ufc/story/jon-jones-settles-court-case-over-drag-racing-charges-081116
6	http://www.foxsports.com/ufc/story/jon-jones-ufc-champion-arrested-police-video-pipe-condoms-found-in-vehicle-050815
6	http://www.foxsports.com/ufc/story/ufc-fines-jon-jones-25-000-after-testing-positive-for-cocaine-011715
6	http://www.foxsports.com/ufc/story/ufc-jon-jones-arrest-warrant-being-issued-felony-charges-hit-and-run-accident-042715
6	http://www.huffingtonpost.com/entry/jon-jones-sentenced-hit-and-run_us_560ac699e4b0af3706de0ca8
6	http://www.koat.com/article/bones-jones-receives-anonymous-calls-after-arrest-1/5063807
6	http://www.latimes.com/sports/sportsnow/la-sp-sn-ufc-fines-jon-jones-cocaine-20150117-story.html
6	http://www.mmaweekly.com/jon-jones-recent-citations-stemmed-from-driving-75-mph-in-a-35-mph-zone
6	http://www.mmaweekly.com/jon-jones-will-not-face-formal-probation-violation-due-to-traffic-incident
6	http://www.sherdog.com/news/news/Dana-White-on-Jon-Jones-Cocaine-Use-The-Stuff-He-Was-Doing-It-Hurts-You-79909
6	http://www.sherdog.com/news/news/Jon-Jones-Pleads-Guilty-to-HitandRun-Charge-Receives-18-Months-Probation-93215
6	http://www.si.com/mma/2015/01/04/jon-jones-defeats-daniel-cormier-ufc-182-legacy
6	http://www.si.com/mma/2015/01/06/jon-jones-cocaine-rehab
6	http://www.usatoday.com/story/sports/ufc/2016/04/19/jon-jones-ufc-197-marijuana-drug-addiction-ovince-saint-preux/83185088/
6	https://sports.vice.com/en_us/article/the-return-of-jon-jones
6	https://www.youtube.com/watch?v=cDzPJcl8nGY
6	https://www.youtube.com/watch?v=e66NfTx4IfI
6	https://www.youtube.com/watch?v=mgYCcw6gilM
6	https://www.youtube.com/watch?v=wYENflmXmGo
7	http://www.foxsports.com/ufc/story/jon-jones-i-totally-had-a-drug-problem-112715
7	http://www.sportingnews.com/other-sports/news/jon-jones-blacked-out-wasted-a-week-before-every-fight/7m9tu0pynnb716lde2zi6bxm4

Photo Credits

The mugshots and photos included in this mini book belong to the Public Domain or are leveraged based on the Fair Use Rationale described below:

- The images are used to depict the subjects which are talked about
- There is no other similar image which is free available

Page	Source
8	*Jackson, Jones and Winklejohn subdued a robber on March 19, 2011* Photo Credit: Twitter
12	*Jon Jones's car crash on May 19, 2012* Photo Credit: WBNG Action News, and Jon Jones
13	*Jon Jones's May 2012 mugshot* Photo Credit: New York Police Department
15	*Officer Martinez's November 2011 Report* Photo Credit: Albuquerque Police Department
16	*Cara Johnson and Michelle Vojtisek* Photo Credit: Instagram and Facebook
25	*Jon Jones's May 2010 Tweet* Photo Credit: Tweeter
33	*Jon Jones' April 2015 Hit-and-Run Accident Diagram* Photo Credit: Albuquerque Police Department
35	*Extract from the Jon Jones's Accident Police Report* Photo Credit: Albuquerque Police Department
35	*Jon Jones's April 2015 Arrest Warrant* Photo Credit: Albuquerque Police Department
36	*Albuquerque Police's April 2015 Tweet* Photo Credit: Tweeter
37	*Jon Jones's April 2015 mugshot* Photo Credit: Bernalillo County Metro Detention Center
44	*Jon Jones's March 24 2016 Police Camera Cam* Photo Credit: Police Department
45	*Jon Jones's March 24 2016 Booking Information* Photo Credit: Bernalillo County Metro Detention Center
46	*Jon Jones's March 2016 mugshot* Photo Credit: Bernalillo County Metro Detention Center
46	*Jon Jones's March 2016 arraignment* Photo Credit: Bernalillo County District Attorney's Office

Appendices

The next pages include reports released to the public by law enforcement agencies and the United States Anti-Doping Agency:

- Jon Jones's January 2011 Car Accident Police Report
- Jon Jones's April 2015 Hit-and-Run Incident Police Report
- Jon Jones's April 2015 Arrest Warrant
- Jon Jones's November 2016 USADA Arbitration Rules Award

Appendix 1: Jon Jones's January 2011 Police Report

Synopsis

On 11/24/11 Jonathan Jones was cited for loss of traction and suspended drivers license and his vehicle was towed at 4900 Jefferson St. NE.

Narrative

On 11/24/11 I observed a black Bentley turn Northbound on Jefferson NE from Westbound McCleod NE. The vehicle came around the corner sideways and tires squealing. The vehicle continued North at a high rate of speed and pulled into the Fantasy World parking lot. I conducted as traffic stop and contacted the driver, identified as Jonathan Jones. I ran Jones drivers license through MVD and it was suspended. I then ran his drivers license through NCIC and they confirmed his it was suspended. Jones was cited for loss of traction and suspended drivers license. Jones vehicle was towed from the scene.

Reporting Officer: MARTINEZ, DOMINIC P. — P1C — P5212 — 11-24-2011
Approving Officer: COTTRELL, ZAKARY — P5412 — 11-27-2011

Appendix 2: Jon Jones's April 2015 Hit-and-Run Police Report

Reporting Department:	ALBUQUERQUE POLICE DEPT	
Crash Report Number:	710246066	
Case Number:	150036411	
Private Property?	YES	
Injury	✓	
Hit and Run?	YES	
Crash Date:	04/26/2015	
Military Time:	11:22	
City Occurred In:	ALBUQUERQUE	
County:	BERNALILLO	
Day of Week:	SUNDAY	
Occurred On:	SOUTHERN AVE SE	
At Intersection With:	JUAN TABO BLVD SE	
Tribal Land?	NO	
Crash Occurred:	ON ROADWAY	
Crash Classification:	OTHER VEHICLE	
Analysis Code:	18 - ONE LEFT TURN/FROM OPP DIR	

Vehicle No. 001

Unit Direction Headed	EAST
On	SOUTHERN AVE SE
Left the Scene of the Crash?	NO
Posted Speed	40
Safe Speed	40
Driver's License State	NM
Type	D
Status	V
Expires	02/13/2022
City	LOS LUNAS
State	NM
Zip Code	87031
Seat Pos	LF
Age	25
Sex	F
Race	H
Injury Code	C
OP Code	6
OP Used Property	YES
Airbag Deployed	B
Ejected	N
Veh. Year	2010
Vehicle Make	HONDA
Color	BURGUNDY (PURPLE) - M
Body Style	PC
Cargo Body Type	OT
Veh. Use	OS
Veh. Use	P
Veh. Towed?	YES
Vehicle Disabled	YES
Damage Severity	HEAVY
Damage Area	11, 10, 9, 8, 7
Extent	DISABLED
Extent	08, 09, 10, 11, 12
Lic. Year	2016
State	NM
Towed By	DANLAR NORTH, LLC
Towed To	102 ALAMEDA BLVD. NW ALBUQUER
HazMat Released	NO
Owner's City	LOS LUNAS
State	NM
Owner Zip	87031
Insured By:	ID PROPERTY CASUALTY

STATE OF NEW MEXICO UNIFORM CRASH REPORT
NM STATUTE 66-7-209
NMDOT COPY

Vehicle No. 002

VEHICLE NO. HEADED	02
Unit Direction	NORTH
On	JUAN TABO BLVD SE
Left the Scene of the Crash?	NO
Posted Speed	40
Safe Speed	40
Driver's License State	NM
Type	D
Status	V
Expires	04/18/2018
City	ALBUQUERQUE
State	NM
Zip Code	87123

Occupants

Seat Pos	Address	City	State	Zip	Age	Sex	Race	Injury Code	OP Code	CP Used Properly	Airbag Deploy	Ejected	EMS Num	Med Trans
LF					38	M	H	O	6	YES	N	N		
LR	SAME	ALBUQUERQUE	NM	87123	10	F	H	O	6	YES	N	N		
RF	SAME	ALBUQUERQUE	NM	87123	8	F	H	O	6	YES	N	N		
RR					10	M	H	O	6	YES	N	N		

Vehicle Details

Veh. Year	2013
Vehicle Make	TOYOTA
Color	TAN - TAN
Body Style	PC
Cargo Body Type	OT
Veh. Use	IB
Veh. Use	P
Veh. Towed	NO
Vehicle Disabled	NO
Lic. Year	2016
State	NM
Damage Severity	MODERATE
Damage Area	12
Extent Appearance	12,19,01

Owner / Insurance

Owner's City	ALBUQUERQUE
Status	NM
Owner Zip	87123
Insured By	USAA

STATE OF NEW MEXICO UNIFORM CRASH REPORT
NM STATUTE 66-7-209
NMDOT COPY

Crash Report Number: 710246006
Case Number: 160036411
Sheet 2 Of 6

VEHICLE NO. 003

Unit Direction HEADED	SOUTH
On	JUAN TABO BLVD SE
Left the Scene of the Crash?	YES
Posted Speed	40
Safe Speed	40

Driver Information: (blank)

Seat Pos: LF

Vehicle Details

Veh. Year	2015
Vehicle Make	BUICK
Color	SILVER - SIL
Body Style	SV
Cargo Body Type	OT
Veh. Use	IB
Veh. Use	P
Veh. Towed?	YES
Vehicle Disabled	YES
Damage Severity	HEAVY
Damage Area	12
Lic. Year	2015
State	NM
License Plate Number	GRF4390
VIN	5GAKVBKD2FJ105830
Extent	DISABLED
	12,11,19,02,01

Towed By: DANLAR NORTH, LLC
Towed To: 102 ALAMEDA BLVD, NW ALBUQUER

HazMat Released: NO

Owner Information

Owner's Last Name	EAN HOLDING
Owner's First Name	EAN HOLDING
Owner's Company Name	ENTERPRISE
Owner's City	ALBUQUERQUE
State	NM
Owner Zip	87112

Road/Conditions

Lighting	DAYLIGHT
Weather	CLEAR
Road Character	STRAIGHT
Road Grade	LEVEL
VEH NO.	01
Road Condition	DRY
Road Surface	PAVED CENTER AND EDGE LIN
Traffic Control	TRAFFIC SIGNALS
Road Lanes	2 LANES
Road Design Div	PHYSICAL DIVID
Road Design	FULL ACCESS CT

Apparent Contributing Factors: NONE

Driver's Actions: GOING STRAIGHT

Sequence of Events

FIRST EVENT	MVT
SECOND EVENT	MVT
THIRD EVENT	MVT
FOURTH EVENT	MVT

Crash Report Number: 710246066
Case Number: 150036411

STATE OF NEW MEXICO UNIFORM CRASH REPORT
NM STATUTE 66-7-209
NMDOT COPY

Sheet 3 Of 6

DRIVER

DRIVER/PEDESTRIAN/PEDALCYCLIST SOBRIETY	DRIVER/PED/PEDALCYCLIST PHYSICAL CONDITION	PEDESTRIAN/PEDALCYCLIST ACTION
HAD NOT CONSUMED ALCOHOL	NO APP. DEFECTS	At Intersection / Not At Intersection / Pedestrian Action - Other
Breath Test Results	Driver Physical Condition - Other	

ROAD

VEH NO.	Road Condition	Road Surface	Traffic Control	Road Lanes	Road Design Div	Road Design
02	DRY	PAVED CENTER AND EDGE LIN	TRAFFIC SIGNALS	2 LANES	PAINTED DIVIDE	FULL ACCESS CT

EVENT

APPARENT CONTRIBUTING FACTORS	DRIVER'S ACTIONS	SEQUENCE OF EVENTS
NONE	STOPPED FOR SIGN/SIGNAL	FIRST EVENT: MVT SECOND EVENT: MVT THIRD EVENT: MVT FOURTH EVENT: MVT

DRIVER

DRIVER/PEDESTRIAN/PEDALCYCLIST SOBRIETY	DRIVER/PED/PEDALCYCLIST PHYSICAL CONDITION	PEDESTRIAN/PEDALCYCLIST ACTION
HAD NOT CONSUMED ALCOHOL	NO APP. DEFECTS	At Intersection / Not At Intersection / Pedestrian Action - Other
Breath Test Results	Driver Physical Condition - Other	

ROAD

VEH NO.	Road Condition	Road Surface	Traffic Control	Road Lanes	Road Design Div	Road Design
03	DRY	PAVED CENTER AND EDGE LIN	TRAFFIC SIGNALS	2 LANES	PAINTED DIVIDE	FULL ACCESS CT

EVENT

APPARENT CONTRIBUTING FACTORS	DRIVER'S ACTIONS	SEQUENCE OF EVENTS
AVOID NO CONTACT - OTHER, AVOID NO CONTACT VEHICLE, DISREGARDED TRAFFIC SIGNAL, DRIVER INATTENTION, EXCESSIVE SPEED, MADE IMPROPER TURN, OTHER IMPROPER DRIVING, UNDER INFLUENCE OF DRUGS OR MEDICATION	LEFT TURN	FIRST EVENT: MVT SECOND EVENT: MVT THIRD EVENT: MVT FOURTH EVENT: MVT

DRIVER

DRIVER/PEDESTRIAN/PEDALCYCLIST SOBRIETY	DRIVER/PED/PEDALCYCLIST PHYSICAL CONDITION	PEDESTRIAN/PEDALCYCLIST ACTION
SOBRIETY UNKNOWN	NO APP. DEFECTS	At Intersection / Not At Intersection / Pedestrian Action - Other
Breath Test Results	Driver Physical Condition - Other	

NARRATIVE

ON 04/26/2015, OFC. J. BRIONEZ AND I WERE DISPATCHED TO A HIT AND RUN TRAFFIC ACCIDENT, AT THE INTERSECTION OF JUAN TABO AND SOUTHERN. CALLER STATED THE DRIVER OF A SILVER SUV RAN FROM THE ACCIDENT. OFC. BRIONEZ AND I ARRIVED, WITH RESCUE ARRIVING ON SCENE SHORTLY AFTER. THE DRIVER OF BOTH VEHICLES REFUSED RESCUE. THE DRIVER OF THE HONDA STATED HER HUSBAND WILL TAKE HER. DRIVER ONE STATED SHE WAS HEADING EAST IN LANE 2, AND WAS CROSSING THOUGH JUAN TABO ON A GREEN LIGHT, WHEN DRIVER 3 RAN THE LIGHT HITTING HER ON THE DRIVER SIDE. DRIVER 2 STATED HE WAS WAITING AT A RED LIGHT FACING NORTH ON JUAN TABO AT SOUTHERN. DRIVER 2 STATED WHEN DRIVER 1 WAS CROSSING ON A GREEN LIGHT, DRIVER 3 TURNED INTO HER FROM THE SOUTHBOUND TURN LANE OF SOUTHERN HITTING HER DRIVER SIDE. WITNESSES AND DRIVERS FROM BOTH VEHICLES, STATED DRIVER OF VEHICLE 3 GOT OUT AND LEFT RUNNING. WITNESSES STATED THE DRIVER OF VEHICLE 3, EXITED AFTER HITTING THE HONDA AND WAS IDENTIFIED AS A BLACK MALE, WEARING A WHITE BUTTON UP SHIRT, WITH DARK PANTS ON AND RAN ONTO A HILL JUST EAST OF THE ACCIDENT. WITNESSES STATED HE SLOUCHED OVER AND RAN BACK TO THE VEHICLE GRABBING A LARGE HAND FULL OF CASH. WITNESSES STATED HE SHOVED THE CASH INTO HIS PANTS AND RAN NORTH JUMPING THE FENCE INTO TERRACITA. I SENT OFFICERS TO ATTEMPT TO LOCATE THE DRIVER OF VEHICLE 3. THE OFFICERS WHO ATTEMPTED TO LOOK FOR HIM, WERE UN SUCCESSFUL. DRIVER 1 WAS TAKEN TO KASEMAN HOSPITAL DUE TO BEING PREGNANT AND FEELING LIKE SHE WAS GOING TO PASS OUT. OFC. BRIONEZ AND I CONDUCTED A SEARCH INCIDENT TO TOW ON THE BUICK. OFC. BRIONEZ FOUND A MARIJUANA PIPE, WITH MARIJUANA INSIDE OF IT, AND TAGGED IT INTO EVIDENCE. I LOCATED PAPERWORK BELONGING TO A JONATHAN JONES, WHICH HAD MMA INFORMATION ON IT. I WAS ABLE TO LOCATE A PHONE NUMBER FOR JON JONES AND PLACED SEVERAL PHONE CALLS WITH NO SUCCESS. I LEFT A MESSAGE FOR JON JONES TO CALL DISPATCH, BUT NEVER RECEIVED ONE. THE PAPERWORK, WILL BE TAGGED INTO EVIDENCE.

Crash Report Number: 710248066
Case Number: 150036411

STATE OF NEW MEXICO UNIFORM CRASH REPORT
NM STATUTE 66-7-209
NMDOT COPY

Sheet 4 Of 6

Other Property Involved	Type	Description of Property and Damage						
	Owner's Last Name		Owner's First Name			Owner's Middle Name		
	Owner's Street Address		Owner's City		State	Zip Code	Owner's Phone	

WITNESS	Witness's Last Name		Witness's First Name			Witness's Middle Name		Age
	Witness's Street Address		Witness's City UNKNOWN		State NM	Zip Code 87123	Witness's Phone	

ENFORCEMENT ACTION - VIOLATIONS

VEH NO.	Last Name	First Name	Middle Name	Violation (Common Name)	Action

Time Notified 11:24	Time Arrived 11:25	Notified By DISPATCH	Supervisor at Scene SGT. FINCHER		Checked By		
Officer's Signature			Officer's Name BENAVIDEZ, T.	Rank P1/C	ID Number 5383	District 521	Report Date 04/26/2015

Crash Report Number: 710248066
Case Number: 150036411

STATE OF NEW MEXICO UNIFORM CRASH REPORT
NM STATUTE 66-7-209
NMDOT COPY

Sheet 5 Of 6

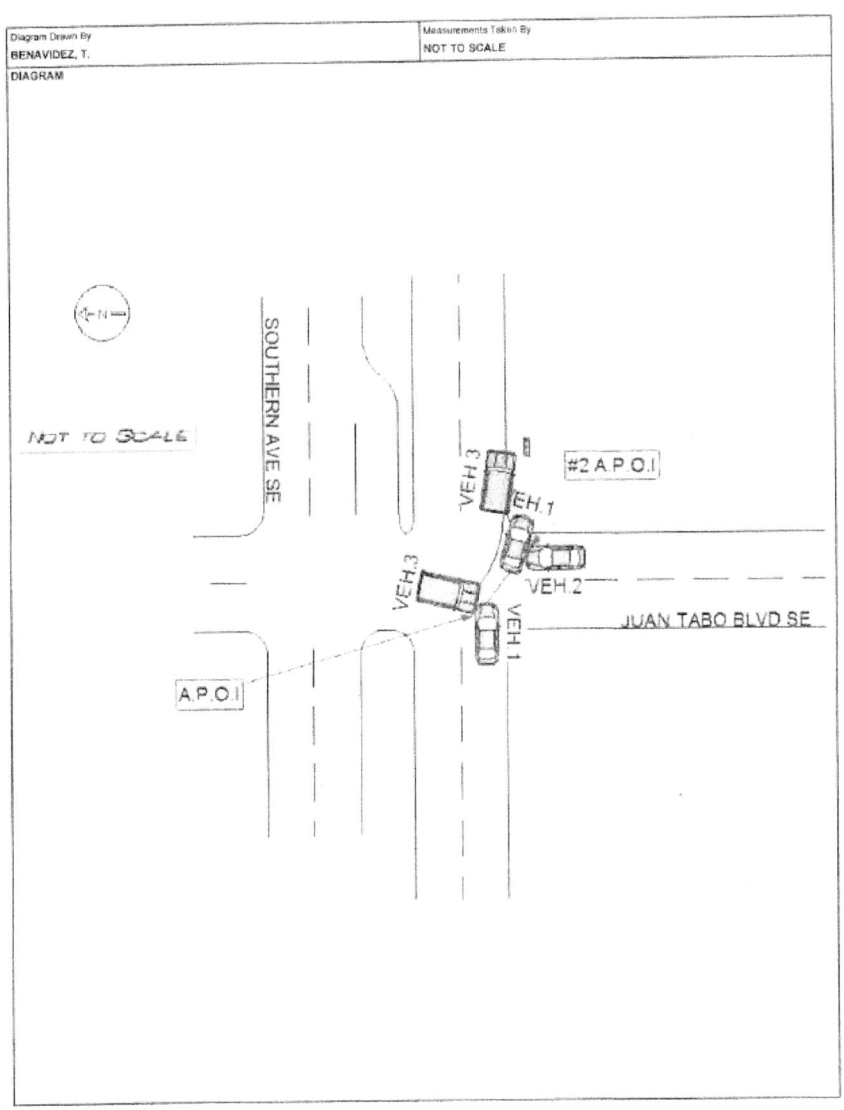

Diagram Drawn By	Measurements Taken By
BENAVIDEZ, T.	NOT TO SCALE
DIAGRAM	

Diagram: Intersection of Southern Ave SE and Juan Tabo Blvd SE, not to scale. Shows vehicles VEH.1, VEH.2, and VEH.3 with A.P.O.I. and #2 A.P.O.I. markers. North arrow indicated.

Crash Report Number: 710246066	STATE OF NEW MEXICO UNIFORM CRASH REPORT	Sheet 6 Of 6
Case Number: 150036411	NM STATUTE 66-7-209 NMDOT COPY	

STATE OF NEW MEXICO UNIFORM CRASH REPORT - SUPPLEMENTAL NARRATIVE

Crash Date	Crash Time	Crash Report Number	Agency Case Number		
04/26/2015	11:22	710246066	150036411		
Officer/Person Submitting Supplemental Report			Rank	ID Number	District	Report Date
BENAVIDEZ, T.			P1/C	5383	523	04/26/2015

NARRATIVE

ON 04/26/2015, OFC. J. BRIONEZ AND I WERE DISPATCHED TO A HIT AND RUN TRAFFIC ACCIDENT, AT THE INTERSECTION OF JUAN TABO AND SOUTHERN. CALLER STATED THE DRIVER OF A SILVER SUV RAN FROM THE ACCIDENT. OFC. BRIONEZ AND I ARRIVED, WITH RESCUE ARRIVING ON SCENE SHORTLY AFTER. THE DRIVER OF BOTH VEHICLES REFUSED RESCUE. THE DRIVER OF THE HONDA STATED HER HUSBAND WILL TAKE HER. DRIVER ONE STATED SHE WAS HEADING EAST IN LANE 2, AND WAS CROSSING THOUGH JUAN TABO ON A GREEN LIGHT, WHEN DRIVER 3 RAN THE LIGHT HITTING HER ON THE DRIVER SIDE. DRIVER 2 STATED HE WAS WAITING AT A RED LIGHT FACING NORTH ON JUAN TABO AT SOUTHERN. DRIVER 2 STATED WHEN DRIVER 1 WAS CROSSING ON A GREEN LIGHT, DRIVER 3 TURNED INTO HER FROM THE SOUTHBOUND TURN LANE OF SOUTHERN HITTING HER DRIVER SIDE. WITNESSES AND DRIVERS FROM BOTH VEHICLES, STATED DRIVER OF VEHICLE 3 GOT OUT AND LEFT RUNNING. WITNESSES STATED THE DRIVER OF VEHICLE 3, EXITED AFTER HITTING THE HONDA AND WAS IDENTIFIED AS A BLACK MALE, WEARING A WHITE BUTTON UP SHIRT, WITH DARK PANTS ON AND RAN ONTO A HILL JUST EAST OF THE ACCIDENT. WITNESSES STATED HE SLOUCHED OVER AND RAN BACK TO THE VEHICLE GRABBING A LARGE HAND FULL OF CASH. WITNESSES STATED HE SHOVED THE CASH INTO HIS PANTS AND RAN NORTH JUMPING THE FENCE INTO TERRACITA. I SENT OFFICERS TO ATTEMPT TO LOCATE THE DRIVER OF VEHICLE 3. THE OFFICERS WHO ATTEMPTED TO LOOK FOR HIM, WERE UN SUCCESSFUL. DRIVER 1 WAS TAKEN TO KASEMAN HOSPITAL DUE TO BEING PREGNANT AND FEELING LIKE SHE WAS GOING TO PASS OUT. OFC. BRIONEZ AND I CONDUCTED A SEARCH INCIDENT TO TOW ON THE BUICK. OFC. BRIONEZ FOUND A MARIJUANA PIPE, WITH MARIJUANA INSIDE OF IT, AND TAGGED IT INTO EVIDENCE. I LOCATED PAPERWORK BELONGING TO A JONATHAN JONES, WHICH HAD MMA INFORMATION ON IT FROM THE STATE OF NEVADA. I WAS ABLE TO LOCATE A PHONE NUMBER FOR JON JONES AND PLACED SEVERAL PHONE CALLS WITH NO SUCCESS. I LEFT A MESSAGE FOR JON JONES TO CALL DISPATCH, BUT NEVER RECEIVED ONE. THE PAPERWORK, WILL BE TAGGED INTO EVIDENCE. THERE WERE ALSO ENTERPRISE RENT A CAR PAPERWORK INSIDE THE VEHICLE, FOR THE LOCATION AT LOMAS AND EASTERDAY. I MADE CONTACT WITH AN UNIDENTIFIED EMPLOYEE, WHO STATED THEY WERE CLOSED AND NOT OPEN UNTIL MONDAY. I WAS CONTACTED BY OFC. J. SULLIVAN, WHO INFORMED ME HE WAS DRIVING EAST ON SOUTHERN AND SEEN THE ACCIDENT, OFF DUTY. OFC. SULLIVAN STATED HE WITNESSED JONATHAN JONES THE MMA FIGHTER EXIT THE SILVER BUICK AND RUN UP A DIRT HILL JUST EAST. OFC. SULLIVAN STATED JON JONES WAS WEARING A WHITE NICE POLO STYLE SHIRT, WITH DARK SLACKS OR JEANS. OFC. SULLIVAN STATED HE WATCHED JON JONES RUN BACK TO THE BUICK AND LOST SIGHT OF HIM AT THIS POINT.

Appendix 3: Jon Jones's April 2015 Arrest Warrant Affidavit

STATE OF NEW MEXICO
-vs-

ARTICLE 2
INITIATION OF PROCEEDINGS
**STATE OF NEW MEXICO
COUNTY OF BERNALILLO
IN THE METROPOLITAN COURT**

Name: Jonathan Jones
Address: ▓▓▓▓▓▓▓▓▓▓▓
Albuquerque, NM 87111
D.O.B. ▓▓▓▓▓▓▓▓
S.S.N. unknown
Charge: Leaving the scene of an accident involving death or personal injuries.

Arrest Date:
Driver Lic. #: ▓▓▓▓▓▓▓▓▓▓▓
Citation #:
Arrest #:
Docket #:
Date Filed: 04/27/2015

Complainant or Officer: Det. T. Benavidez   Man #: 5383

CRIMINAL COMPLAINT- ARREST WARRANT AFFIDAVIT

The undersigned, under penalty of perjury, complains and says that on or about the 27th day of April 20 15, in the County of Bernalillo, State of New Mexico, the above-named defendant(s) did (here state the essential facts):

The affiant, Tommy L. Benavidez, is a full-time, sworn law enforcement officer with the Albuquerque Police Department. I have been a full time, sworn law enforcement officer since October 2009. I attended and completed the basic police academy offered by the Albuquerque Police Department. Since my commission, I have served in the Field Services Bureau, Patrol Division. For the last five years, I have been assigned to bicycle patrol in the Foothills Area Command. Currently, I am assigned on a temporary assignment to the Foothills Impact Team.

During my tenure as a career police officer, I have received training and on-the job experience related to the investigation of numerous types of crimes including, but not limited to, investigation of crimes against persons and property, to include; homicides, assaults, child abuse, weapons offenses, burglaries, various types of thefts, narcotics and narcotics-related crimes. I have received training related to the identification of many different types of controlled substances, including marijuana, methamphetamine/amphetamine, heroin, cocaine/crack cocaine, as well as other various drugs, along with the methods of use, sales, delivery, concealment, possession and manufacture these controlled substances.

On 04/26/2015, Ofc. J. Brionez and I were dispatched to a traffic accident with injuries at the intersection of Juan Tabo and Southern. The call stated there were three vehicles involved, with possible air bag deployment. A silver Buick SUV, tan Toyota Camry and a maroon Honda were the vehicles reported to be involved. Callers advised that a male driver ran north bound Juan Tabo, wearing a long sleeve button down shirt.

Ofc. Brionez arrived on scene first, advising a 30 yr old female was pregnant and complaining of wrist injuries. Ofc. Brionez advised a Bernalillo County Sherriff Deputy was on scene. Ofc. Brionez started a tow truck for three vehicles.

I arrived on scene and observed three vehicles, which seem to be disabled. I made contact with the two remaining drivers, who refused transport by rescue. I made contact with the female driver, identified as Vanessa Sonnenberg, who stated, "my husband will take me to the hospital." Vanessa stated she was driving east on Southern, and was crossing through Juan Tabo, on a green light. As she was crossing through, the driver of the silver SUV ran the red light, and hit her on the driver's side. I asked Vanessa if she was going to go to the hospital. Vanessa replied "I am pregnant and I feel like I am going to pass out. My arm is hurting all the way up and my husband is going to take me to the hospital." I spoke with the driver of the tan Toyota, identified as Falsen Cambre. Falsen explained he was at a red light, facing north on Juan Tabo at Southern. He observed the Honda, attempting to go through the green light east at Juan Tabo. Falsen observed the silver Buick turn directly into the red Honda crashing into her driver's side. Falsen advised the Honda was pushed into his vehicle, damaging the front end and the silver Buick came to a stop just east.

I contacted a witness, identified as Bruce Benson, who left his information with officers at the scene before he left. Bruce advised he stopped to check on the driver of the Buick, who he observed as a black male in the driver's seat. Bruce repeatedly asked the driver if he needed any help. Bruce stated "the driver continued to ignore him over and over." Eventually the driver got out of the silver Buick and jogged on top of the dirt hill to the east. Bruce observed the male slouch over; however, a few minutes later, the driver came back to the vehicle. Bruce stated he told the driver "You should sit down in case you're hurt. Police are on their way." The driver continued to ignore him retrieved cash from the vehicle and shoved it into his pockets. The driver fled the area, running past Bruce, north into the gated community.

The off duty deputy, K. Woods, advised he was driving east on Southern approaching Juan Tabo. Deputy Woods observed a traffic accident and stopped to check on injuries. Deputy Woods blocked traffic to protect the scene, exited the patrol unit and checked on the driver of the maroon vehicle. After checking on the driver he contacted the witness, Bruce Benson, who was parked in front of the silver Buick. Bruce told Deputy Woods the driver of the silver Buick was a black male, and was wearing a white shirt with slacks. Deputy Woods remained on scene until field units relieved him.

I was contacted by Ofc. J. Sullivan. Ofc. Sullivan explained he was off duty driving north on Juan Tabo approaching Southern. He was preparing to turn east on Southern from Juan Tabo, when he was slowed due to a car in front of him. Ofc. Sullivan came to a complete stop behind another vehicle in the east bound turn lane, just east of the silver Buick. Ofc. Sullivan observed the traffic accident scene and noticed a male standing at the driver's door area of the Buick. Ofc. Sullivan immediately recognized the male to Mixed Martial Arts (MMA) fighter Jon Jones. Ofc. Sullivan stated "Jon Jones was wearing a nice white polo style shirt, with either dark jeans or slacks on." Ofc. Sullivan thought to himself "oh man, that's Jon Jones." He observed Jon Jones jog in front of the vehicle stopped in front of him, and up the dirt hill on the south east corner of Juan Tabo and Southern. After a few minutes, Jon Jones jogged back to the silver Buick, and entered the vehicle from the driver's door. I asked Ofc. Sullivan how he knew it was Jon Jones, to which Ofc. Sullivan replied, "I watch UFC all the time, I know what Jon Jones looks like."

I attempted several phone calls to Jonathan Jones from the foothills substation. I left two voicemails advising Jon Jones to call dispatch and ask for me to call him back. I did not receive any phone calls or messages from Jonathan Jones.

I contacted Vanessa to get an update on her injuries. Vanessa stated she went to Kaseman hospital and was told she had a fractured arm and wrist. Vanessa advised me she is in a sling now and that she receives her cast tomorrow. Vanessa stated she was on her way to get an ultra sound today.

BASED ON THE AFOREMENTIONED FACTS, I RESPECTFULLY REQUEST THAT AN ARREST WARRANT BE ISSUED FOR **Jonathan Jones** ON THE LISTED FELONY CHARGE.

contrary to Section(s) __66-7-201c__ _____ NMSA 1978.
I SWEAR OR AFFIRM UNDER PENALTY OF PERJURY THAT THE FACTS SET FORTH ABOVE ARE TRUE TO THE BEST OF MY INFORMATION AND BELIEF. I UNDERSTAND THAT IT IS A CRIMINAL OFFENSE SUBJECT TO THE PENALTY OF IMPRISONMENT TO MAKE A FALSE STATEMENT IN A CRIMINAL COMPLAINT.

SUBSCRIBED AND SWORN TO ME IN THE ABOVE NAMED COUNTY OF THE STATE OF NEW MEXICO THIS _____ DAY OF _____, 2015 AT _____.

_____
JUDGE, NOTARY, OR OTHER OFFICER
AUTHORIZED TO ADMINISTER OATHS

AFFIANT

DATE

DATE   MAN#

ASSISTANT DISTRICT ATTORNEY   DATE

APD CAD OR CASE#

CF001
METROPOLITAN COURT RULE 7-201

Approved: Supreme Court, October 1, 1974; amended effective September 1, 1990; April 1, 1991; November 1, 1991.
❏ - Court   ❏ - Defendant   ❏ - Attorney   ❏ - District Attorney

Appendix 4: Jon Jones's November 2016 Arbitration Ruling

ARBITRATION AWARD PURSUANT TO THE UFC ARBITRATION RULES

JON JONES, Applicant,

vs.

UNITED STATES ANTI-DOPING AGENCY ("USADA"), Respondent.

AWARD

1. INTRODUCTION

1.1. In this, the inaugural proceeding before the UFC Arbitration Panel the issue is as to the appropriate sanction under the UFC ADP rules for an admitted anti-doping policy violation ("ADPV") by Jon Jones ("the Applicant").

1.2. Applicant contends that he took a product, which he believed to be a pill of "Cialis"; a medicine whose absence from the WADA prohibited list he had previously checked with his agent, but which unbeknown, indeed unknowable, by him, was contaminated. Therefore he bore, he asserts, at most a light degree of fault in taking it. USADA ("the Respondent") does not accept that explanation and in any event asserts that the Applicant's fault was significant.

1.3. Cialis is itself not a prohibited substance but a legitimate erectile dysfunction medication; its purpose is to enhance sexual not sporting performance. It is manufactured by the well-known pharmacist Eli Lilly and is the brand name of its active agent Tadalafil.

1.4. The product that the Applicant claims to have taken was also called Tadalafil and purported to have the same properties. It was, however, manufactured by the company selling under the name "AllAmericanPeptide.com" ("All American Peptide") to standards far less rigorous than those required by the US Food and Drugs Administration ("the FDA").

2. THE PARTIES

2.1. The Applicant is a 29-year old mixed martial art (MMA) fighter, with a record of 29-1. He is a former UFC light heavyweight champion, and current interim light heavyweight champion. He was ranked as the # 1 light heavyweight fighter in the world by various media outlets for a number of years, and was also ranked the # 1 pound-for-pound fighter in the world by multiple publications. He lives in Albuquerque, New Mexico. The Applicant is represented by Mr. Howard L. Jacobs, attorney-at-law, Westlaw Village, CA.

2.2. The Respondent is an independent, non-profit, non-governmental agency whose sole mission is to preserve the integrity of competition, inspire true sport and protect the rights of clean athletes. It independently administers the year-round, anti-doping program for the Ultimate Fighting Championship ("UFC"), which includes the in- and out-of-competition testing of all UFC athletes. The Respondent is represented by Mr. William Bock III and Mr. Onye Ikwuakor, counsels for the USADA, in Colorado Springs, CO.

3. MATTERS SUBJECT TO ARBITRATION

3.1. FC has adopted the rules, policies and procedures set forth in the UFC Anti-Doping Policy. Any asserted anti-doping policy violation arising out of the policy or an asserted violation of the anti-doping rules set forth in that policy shall be resolved through the Results Management Process described in the policy and the pertinent arbitration rules ("the Arbitration Rules") adopted by the UFC.

3.2. rbitration pursuant to the Arbitration Rules shall be the exclusive forum for any appeal or any complaint by any athlete to (i) appeal or contest USADA's assertion of an anti-doping policy violation or (ii) any dispute that the UFC or USADA and the Chief Arbitrator determine is one over which the UFC has jurisdiction and standing and the Chief Arbitrator has agreed to appoint an arbitrator.

3.3. FC has in the Arbitration Rules selected McLaren Global Sports Solutions Inc. ("MGSS") to administer those Arbitration Rules.

3.4.   On September 29, 2016, Mr. Jacobs on behalf of the Applicant requested MGSS to submit his client's case to arbitration pursuant to the Arbitration Rules.

3.5.   Consequently on 18 October 2016, a panel of three arbitrators consisting of Mr. Michael Beloff QC (Chairman) of London, UK, Mr. Markus Manninen of Helsinki, Finland and Mr. Lars Halgreen of Copenhagen, Denmark ("the Panel") was appointed by MGSS.

4.   FACTUAL BACKGROUND

4.1.   On July 1, 2015, the UFC ADP entered into force and USADA became the independent administrator of the UFC Anti-Doping Program. USADA states that "the first three months of the program are primarily focused on ensuring UFC athletes have received the necessary education to understand their rights and responsibilities, under the new anti-doping program."

4.2.   On September 11, 2015, USADA added the Applicant to the UFC RTP, thereby requiring him to complete an online educational tutorial and regularly to provide USADA with his whereabouts information in order to allow USADA to locate him for no advance notice out-of-competition testing.

4.3.   On October 8, 2015, the Applicant completed the 2015 online educational tutorial for new athletes in the UFC Anti-Doping Program and on December 22, 2015, acknowledged "I understand the material covered in this course."

4.4.   On December 8, 2015, USADA tested the Applicant for the first time. The Applicant did not declare the use of any substances during the sample collection process. The test was negative.

4.5.   On December 22, 2015, the Applicant completed the 2016 online educational tutorial for returning athletes in the UFC Anti-Doping Program.

4.6. On March 4, 2016, USADA tested the Applicant for the second time. The Applicant did not declare the use of any substances during the sample collection process. The test was negative.

4.7. On March 25, 2016, USADA tested the Applicant for the third time. The Applicant did not declare the use of any substances during the sample collection process. The test was negative.

4.8. On April 4, 2016, USADA tested the Applicant for the fourth time. The Applicant did not declare the use of any substances during the sample collection process. The test was negative.

4.9. On April 23, 2016, USADA tested the Applicant for the fifth time, and for the first time in competition. The Applicant declared the use of eight (8) different substances (all World Anti- Doping Code ("WADC") compliant) during the sample collection process. The test was negative.

4.10. On June 16, 2016, USADA tested the Applicant for the sixth time (and out of competition). The Applicant was located for testing based on the whereabouts information he had submitted to USADA in his quarterly Whereabouts Filing. The Applicant was officially notified for testing at 7:45 a.m., and subsequently provided urine Sample #1584598 ("the Sample") in accordance with the UFC ADP.

4.11. At the time of the sample collection, on the Applicant's Doping Control Form (June 16, 2106), the Standard Declaration of Use required him to declare, inter alia, "Prescription/non- prescription medications (...) dietary supplements and/or other substances taken in last seven (7) days." The Applicant, however, affirmed that he had no substances to declare (in particular, he made no reference to either Cialis or Tadalafil) and by signing the completed form certified that the information he had given on the document, was correct.

4.12. Following the processing of the Applicant's Sample, it was sent to the World Anti-Doping Agency ("WADA") accredited laboratory in Salt Lake City, Utah (the "Utah Laboratory"), for analysis.

4.13. On July 6, 2016, the Utah Laboratory reported to USADA that the A Sample for urine Sample #1584598, had tested positive for the presence of hydroxyclomiphene (a metabolite of clomiphene) and a letrozole metabolite as shown in the A Sample Confidential Test Report and Laboratory Document Package.

4.14. The same day, USADA notified the Applicant of the adverse finding for the presence of two prohibited substances in his urine Sample, and informed him that a provisional suspension had been imposed against him as a result of his positive test. In that same correspondence, USADA informed the Applicant that the B Sample analysis of his urine Sample #1584598 would take place on July 7, 2016.

4.15. On July 8, 2016, the Utah Laboratory reported to USADA that the analysis of the Applicant's B Sample had confirmed the presence of hydroxyclomiphene and a letrozole metabolite in the Applicant's urine Sample #1584598 as shown in the B Sample Confidential Test Report and Laboratory Document Package.

4.16. That same day, USADA informed the Applicant of the B Sample confirmation and formally charged him with an anti-doping policy violation for the presence of one or more Prohibited Substances (or their markers or metabolites) in his Sample (UFC ADP 2.1) and the Use or Attempted Use (UFC ADP 2.2) of one or more banned performance enhancing drugs. In the Initial Charging Letter, the Applicant was advised that USADA was seeking the standard two (2) year period of ineligibility against him for his doping offenses, and that the sanction could be increased up to a four (4) year period of ineligibility if aggravating circumstances were found.

4.17. On July 22, 2016, USADA informed the Applicant that the potential sanction lengths outlined in the Initial Charging Letter were incorrect and that USADA was seeking a one (1) year, rather than a two (2) year period of ineligibility against him, because his alleged doping violations involved Specified Substances within the meaning of the WADA Prohibited List and Article 4.2.2 of the UFC ADP.

4.18.   In that letter, USADA sought the following sanctions:

- a one year period of ineligibility, beginning on July 6, 2016;
- (at the discretion of UFC) disqualification of any competitive results achieved on or subsequent to June 16, 2016;
- a one year period of ineligibility beginning on July 6, 2016 from participating in any capacity, in any Bout or activity authorized or organized by the UFC, any Athletic Commission(s) or any clubs, member associations or affiliates of Signatories to the World Anti-Doping Code; and
- all other financial consequences which may be imposed by the UFC as set forth in Article 10.10 of the UFC Anti-Doping Policy.

4.19.   In that letter, USADA further advised the Applicant that his period of ineligibility could be up to three (3) years depending upon the applicability of "aggravating circumstances". USADA wrote:

"(...) if it is determined that you are subject to the application of aggravating circumstances as set forth in Article 10.2.3 of the UFC Anti-Doping Policy, your period of ineligibility can be increased up to a three (3) year period of ineligibility as opposed to the standard one (1) year sanction. Aggravating circumstances which can increase your period of ineligibility can be based either on conduct which occurred in connection with the violation or on conduct which occurred subsequently, through the conclusion of any disciplinary proceedings. For example, untruthfulness or other misconduct before a hearing panel constitutes aggravating circumstances which can increase your period of ineligibility."

4.20.   On or about 25 July 2016 the Applicant's attorney sent (i) a sealed silver pouch of Tadalafil of the kind said to have been ingested by the Applicant, (ii) a bottle of T-Anabol, a WADC compliant product that he had been taking since 2011, to Korva laboratories.

4.21.   The former was processed in August 2016 and tested positive for clomiphene and letrozole. The latter was processed on an unknown date and tested negative for those substances.

4.22. On August 5, 2016, the Applicant requested a hearing under the UFC ADP and UFC Arbitration Rules.

4.23. On or about August 5, 2016, the Applicant's attorney advised USADA that it had been determined that the source of the prohibited substances in Applicant's Sample was a product called Tadalafil, which had been obtained from the online retailer AllAmericanPeptide by Applicant's training partner, Eric Blasich. Thereafter, USADA arranged for the Utah Laboratory to conduct testing on independently acquired packages of Tadalafil, which were ordered from AllAmericanPeptide.com.

4.24. On August 5, 2016, the Utah Laboratory ordered one package of Tadalafil from AllAmericanPeptide.

4.25. On August 8, 2016, USADA ordered one package of Tadalafil from AllAmericanPeptide.

4.26. On August 26, 2016, USADA requested that Applicant's attorney send five (5) capsules from an open package of Tadalafil that was in his possession to the Utah Laboratory for testing, it being USADA's understanding from what it was informed by the Applicant's attorney that the capsule that allegedly caused Applicant's positive test was from that particular package of Tadalafil.

4.27. On August 31, 2016, USADA requested that the Applicant's attorney send additional capsules to the Utah Laboratory because the capsules he had previously sent to the Laboratory were damaged in transit.

4.28. On September 21, 2016, the Applicant's attorney provided USADA with a signed declaration for Eric Blasich. In the declaration, Mr. Blasich stated that he is mixed martial arts fighter and teammate of Applicant. Mr. Blasich also explained that on or about June 14, 2016, he provided Applicant with one capsule of Tadalafil, at the Applicant's request. Mr. Blasich stated that he purchased the product from the web-site AllAmericanPeptide but did not provide any further details.

4.29. On September 21, 2016, the Applicant's attorney also provided USADA with a signed declaration for the Applicant. In the declaration, the Applicant affirmed Mr. Blasich's account concerning how the Tadalafil came to be in his possession and stated that he only used the product on one occasion. The Applicant also explained that he made sure the product was not prohibited under the UFC Anti-Doping Program[1] before using it on the evening of June 14, 2016; but no further details were disclosed of any steps that he took to ensure that the product was safe to use.

4.30. On September 26, 2016, the Utah Laboratory reported that all four of the Tadalafil product shipments it had obtained or received contained clomiphene, letrozole and tamoxifen[2].

4.31. On September 29, 2016, the Applicant, through his attorney, in his UFC Request for Arbitration Form requested an expedited arbitration hearing to be resolved prior to November 10, 2016.

4.32. On October 5, 2016, the parties to this arbitration submitted a joint proposal for an expedited hearing schedule in this matter, in which (i) a one-day hearing would be held in this UFC Anti- Doping Program matter in Los Angeles on October 31, 2016; and (ii) a Reasoned Award would be issued as soon as practical after the conclusion of the Hearing, and in any event no later than 3:00 p.m. EDT on November 9, 2016[3].

4.33. On 7 October 2016 MGSS confirmed this expedited schedule.

4.34. On 31 October 2016 the hearing took place in Santa Monica, California, USA being the seat of arbitration sought by the parties as most convenient and endorsed by the Panel pursuant to Article 7 of the Arbitration Rules.

---

[1] UFC ADP adopts the WADC Prohibited List.
[2] Like clomiphene and letrozole, tamoxifen is a Prohibited Substance in the class of Hormone and Metabolic Modulators on the WADA Prohibited List
[3] When the Applicant faces disciplinary proceedings before the Nevada State Athletic Commission arising out of the same alleged doping office at which, inter alia, his license as a professional mixed martial artist may be at risk.

4.35. The Panel has carefully considered the pre-hearing briefs and the oral evidence given on oath at the hearing by Mr. Malki Kawa, the Applicant's agent, Mr. Blasich and the Applicant himself on behalf of the Applicant and Mr. Jeff Novitsky, Head of UFC Health and Performance Department and Dr. Daniel Eichner, Head of the Utah Laboratory on behalf of the Respondent, as well as the submissions made by Howard Jacobs, for the Applicant and William Bock, III and C. Onye Ikwuakor for the Respondent. The Panel has directed itself in accordance with the UFC ADP Rules, the Arbitration Rules and the laws of the State of Nevada (the Arbitration Rules Article 15).

5. UFC ADP RULES

5.1. UFC ADP rules provide, so far as material, as follows: "The following constitute Anti-Doping Policy Violations:

> 2.1 Presence of a Prohibited Substance or its Metabolites or Markers in an Athlete's Sample.
>
> . . . .
>
> 10.2 Ineligibility for Presence, Use or Attempted Use, or Possession of a Prohibited Substance or Prohibited Method
>
> The period of Ineligibility for a violation of Articles 2.1, 2.2 or 2.6 shall be as follows, subject to potential reduction or suspension pursuant to Articles 10.4,
>
> 10.5 or 10.6 or potential increase in the period of Ineligibility under Article 10.2.3:
>
> 10.2.1 The period of Ineligibility shall be two years where the Anti-Doping Policy Violation involves a non-Specified Substance or Prohibited Method.
>
> 10.2.2 The period of Ineligibility shall be one year where the Anti-Doping Policy Violation involves a Specified Substance.

10.2.3 The period of Ineligibility may be increased up to an additional two years where Aggravating Circumstances[4] are present.

10.5.1 Reduction of Sanctions for Specified Substances[5] or Contaminated Products[6] for Violations of Article 2.1, 2.2 or 2.6

10.5.1.1 Specified substances

Where the Anti-Doping Policy Violation involves a Specified Substance, then the period of Ineligibility shall be, at a minimum, a reprimand and no period of Ineligibility, and at a maximum, the period of Ineligibility set forth in Article 10.2.2, depending on the Athlete's or other Person's degree of Fault.

10.5.1.2 Contaminated Products

In cases where the Athlete or other Person can establish that the detected Prohibited Substance came from a Contaminated Product, then the period of Ineligibility shall be, at a minimum, a reprimand and no period of Ineligibility, and at a maximum, the period of Ineligibility set forth in Article 10.2, depending on the Athlete's or other Person's degree of Fault.

. . . . . .

---

[4] Aggravating Circumstances are defined as "(...) where the Anti-Doping violation was intentional, the Anti-Doping Policy Violation had significant potential to enhance an Athlete's Bout performance, and one of the following additional factors is present: (...) the Athlete (...) Used (...) a Prohibited Substance (...) on multiple occasions; the Athlete (...) engaged in deceptive or obstructing conduct to avoid the detection or adjudication of an Anti-Doping Policy Violation."
[5] Specified Substances are defined as "(...) all prohibited substances (...) except substances in the classes of anabolic agents and hormones, and those stimulants and hormone antagonists and modulators so identified on the Prohibited List (...)"
[6] The definition of "Contaminated Product" is "A product that contains a Prohibited Substance that is not disclosed on the product label or in information available in a reasonable Internet search." This is, somewhat confusingly, not the same as the ordinary meaning of contaminated, i.e. polluted, Oxford English Dictionary definition

10.11 Commencement of Ineligibility Period

Except as provided below, the period of Ineligibility shall start on the date of the final hearing decision providing for Ineligibility (...)

10.11.2 Timely Admission

Where the Athlete (...) promptly (which, in all cases, for an Athlete means before the Athlete Bouts again) admits the Anti-Doping Policy Violation after being confronted with the Anti-Doping Policy Violation by USADA, the period of Ineligibility may start as early as the date of Sample collection or the date on which another Anti-Doping Policy Violation last occurred. In each case, however, where this Article is applied, the Athlete (...) shall serve at least one-half of the period of Ineligibility going forward from the date the Athlete (...) accepted the imposition of a sanction, the date of a hearing decision imposing a sanction, or the date the sanction is otherwise imposed. (...)

10.11.3.1 If a Provisional Suspension is imposed on (...) an Athlete (...) and that Provisional Suspension is respected, then the Athlete (...) shall receive a credit for such period of Provisional Suspension against any period of ineligibility which may ultimately be imposed."

5.2. In short, for an ADPV for a specified substance (or a contaminated product), the standard sanction is a one year period of ineligibility, subject in certain defined circumstances to reduction to no less than a reprimand or in other defined circumstances to increase up to no more than three years. Timely admissions may put back the start of the period. The athlete will be given credit for any period of provisional suspension.

6. ISSUES

6.1. The Applicant does not contend that the sample tested was not his. Neither does he contend that the Utah Laboratory analysis of his Sample was inaccurate or that the laboratory failed to comply in any respect with the International Standard for Laboratories ("ISL").

Accordingly, USADA is entitled to the benefit of the presumption that the laboratory analysis was in accord with the ISL.

6.2 The Applicant does not dispute that the Sample contained metabolites of clomiphene and letrozole, which are Prohibited Substances in the class of Hormones and Metabolic Modulators on the WADC Prohibited List. Letrozole is described on the Prohibited List as an "aromatase inhibitor" and clomiphene is similarly identified as an "anti-estrogenic substance".

6.3. . The UFC ADP expressly states that "presence of a Prohibited Substance or its Metabolites or Markers in the Athlete's A Sample (…) where the Athlete's B Sample is analyzed and the B Sample confirms the presence of the Prohibited Substance or its Metabolites or Markers found in the Athlete's A Sample" is sufficient proof of an anti-doping policy violation", cf. UFC ADP 2.1.2. The presence of clomiphene and letrozole metabolites in Applicant's A and B Samples therefore constitutes an anti-doping policy violation.

6.4. Accordingly, the only remaining issue before this Panel is to determine the appropriate sanction under the UFC ADP for the Applicant's anti-doping policy violation.

6.5. . As to sanction the following issues arise:
- (i) what was the source of the substances ("Source");
- (ii) which UFC ADP rules apply ("Applicable Rules");
- (iii) what was the degree of fault, if any, of the Applicant ("Fault");
- (iv) can the Applicant gain any credit as to start date for a timely admission ("Start Date");
- (v) can the provisional suspension be taken into account ("Provisional Suspension"); and
- (vi) are aggravating circumstances present ("Aggravating Circumstances").

7. SOURCE

7.1. In the Panel's view, proof of precisely how and when the substance got into the athlete's system is a strict threshold requirement of a plea of no (or light) fault, because otherwise it would be impossible to assess the athlete's claim that he bears no (or light) fault for its presence there. See, e.g., Alabbar v. FEI, CAS 2013/A/3124, at para 12.2, quoting with approval WADA v. Stanic & Swiss Olympic Association, CAS 2006/A/1130, at para 39 ("Obviously this precondition is important and necessary; otherwise an athlete's degree of diligence or absence of fault would be examined in relation to circumstances that are speculative and that could be partly or entirely made up. To allow any such speculation as to the circumstances, in which an athlete ingested a prohibited substance would undermine the strict liability rules underlying (...) the World Anti-Doping Code, thereby defeating their purpose"). The fact that the UFC ADP do not, and WADC (2015 edn) no longer, make express reference to such need cannot, in the Panel's view, detract from its conclusion as to the appropriate point of departure for its analysis.

7.2 Furthermore. (i) The Applicant must establish the Source of Prohibited Substances by a balance of probability, cf. UFC ADP Article 3.1. (ii). The Applicant must do so by specific and convincing evidence, rather than mere speculation. See e.g.

- IRB v. Keyter, CAS 2006/A/1067: "One hypothetical source of a positive test does not prove to the level of satisfaction required that [an athlete's explanation for the presence of a prohibited substance in his sample] is factually or scientifically probable. Mere speculation is not proof that it actually did occur. The Respondent has a stringent requirement to offer persuasive evidence of how such contamination occurred." at Paras 6.10-6.11.
- FEI v. Aleksandr Kovshov (FEI 2012/02): "A mere denial of wrongdoing and the advancement of a speculative or innocent explanation are insufficient to meet the Athlete's burden of showing how the Prohibited Substance entered his body. Rather, the Athlete needs to adduce specific and competent evidence that is sufficient to persuade the Tribunal that the explanation advanced is more likely than not to be correct." at Para 18.

7.3. Applicant's explanation can be summarised as follows. In June 2016, in preparation for his UFC 200 title fight with Daniel Cormier he was training with Mr. Blasich, another MMA fighter, at a camp in Albuquerque. On or about June 14, 2016, while they were out at dinner, Mr. Blasich told Applicant that he had been using a product called Cialis. The Applicant – who understood Cialis to be a product like Viagra (which he had previously used) – asked Mr. Blasich who had tablets which he described as Cialis in his car, to give him one. Mr. Blasich did so. The Applicant took the single tablet on the spot.

7.4. tablet which Mr Blasich gave the Applicant was not in fact Cialis but a Tadalafil tablet purchased from the All American Peptide web-site, which was contaminated with the prohibited substances.

7.5. Respondent did not expressly propose an alternative explanation. The literature available to the Panel identifies two reasons why clomiphene or letrozole may be taken by males: firstly to counteract the estrogenic side effects which can be caused by use of anabolic steroids, secondly to enhance natural testosterone production. This was confirmed by Dr. Eichner.

7.6. However, the Respondent did not seek to suggest that the Applicant took the prohibited substances for either of those purposes. Rather, it sought to cast doubt on the Applicant's explanation and submitted that it had not passed the threshold of balance of probabilities, in other words as being more likely than not.

7.7. Panel notes nonetheless that even had the Respondent advanced a positive case of its own as to source, which the Panel had declined to accept, this would not have itself carried the Applicant over the threshold of probability.

7.8. In IWBF v. UKAD & Gibbs (CAS 2010/A/2230) the Sole Arbitrator observed: "Seeking to eliminate by such an approach all alternative hypotheses as to how the substance entered his body and thus to proffer the conclusion that what remains must be the truth reflects the reasoning attributed to the legendary fictional detective Sherlock Holmes by Sir Arthur Conan Doyle in 'The Sign of Four' but is reasoning impermissible for a judicial officer or body. As Lord Brandon[7] said disapproving of such approach in The Popi M 1985 1 WLR 984 a judge (or arbitrator) can always say that 'the party on whom the burden of proof lies in relation to any averment made by him has failed to discharge that burden'. [p. 955]" Nonetheless a decision by an anti-doping agency not to advance any positive case does give a forensic advantage to the athlete, given that if the athlete's (here the Applicant's) explanation for the presence of the prohibited substances in his sample, was not correct there must necessarily be an alternative explanation for that presence.

7.9. The Respondent's chosen assault on the Applicant's explanation has two main prongs. First, the explanation was inconsistent with the main contemporary document, the doping control form, in which the Applicant expressly stated that he "has no substances (...) to declare". Second, the Utah Laboratory had identified in all four sets of Tadalafil tablets sent to it for analyses the presence of tamoxifen, a substance which had not been found in the Applicant's sample, the discrepancy suggesting that he must have taken something other than Tadalafil.

7.10. The first argument lost much of its impetus when, albeit belatedly, Mr. Blasich was able to provide documentation which showed at least that Mr. Blasich had purchased, through a joint account with a close friend and fitness model, a supply of Tadalafil tablets to be delivered to his home address in New York, prior to the 14 June 2016. While this did not of course prove that he did have the tablets with him in Albuquerque or that he gave one to the Applicant, it did at least prove that he could have done so.

7.11. The second depended upon the Utah Laboratory's results for its testing of the Tadalafil samples set out below (concentrations measured in micrograms per capsule):

---

[7] A judge sitting in England's then Highest Court, the Appellate Committee of the House of Lords

Sample # - Source	Clomiphene	Letrozole	Tamoxifen
Sample 1 – Utah Lab	10	170	360
Sample 2 – USADA	130	80	120
Sample 3 – Applicant (broken capsules)	320	37	230
Sample 4 – Applicant (intact capsules)	430	45	320

7.12. 2. The Panel noted, however, the volatility of the concentrations of the substances, for which tests were carried out, between the various samples taken. Given additionally what Dr. Eichner himself regarded as the "sloppiness" of the manufacturing process at All American Peptide, it could not discount the possibility that the Applicant's sample might have contained tamoxifen, but in a concentration so low as to be undetectable by the Utah Laboratory, or indeed that the Applicant had ingested a rogue tablet of Tadalafil which had no tamoxifen at all. (Mr. Jacobs also ventilated the hypothesis that the Utah Laboratory's analysis of the Applicant's sample might have been defective.

As to this, the Panel observes that there was no cogent evidence, relevant to the analysis under consideration, to support such hypothesis.)

7.13. 3. Mr. Bock for the Respondent skilfully and methodically sought to probe other aspects of the Applicant's explanation. He was able to expose some errors, omissions and other disturbing features in the declarations of both the Applicant and Mr. Blasich, each sworn to be true and correct under penalty of perjury. (i) The declarations referred to a dinner on the evening of 14 June "with other teammates" (plural). The oral evidence was that there was only one other person at dinner, their coach Izzy. (ii) Mr. Blasich referred to his own purchase of the tablets from All American Peptide. The oral evidence was that the actual purchaser was Mr. Blasich's friend. (iii) Mr. Blasich had initially provided to the Panel an invoice from All American Peptide for Tadalafil tablets dated 25 May 2016 and said to be the origin of the tablet taken by the Applicant. However, as he accepted, it could not in fact be so, because since it identified a purchase made after he had left New York (where he claimed they had been delivered) in his car to drive to Albuquerque. (iv) The invoice belatedly produced and finally relied on for the same purposes contained an order for clomiphene as well as for Tadalafil. (v) Neither declaration whose drafting appears to have been co-ordinated by Malki Kawa, referred to anything like the detail of their oral statements which were themselves not wholly consistent as to what happened, where and when, on the evening in question. (vi) The Applicant has not been candid on his doping control form and gave different excuses for that lack of candour, embarrassment about disclosure of his use of so called Cialis on the one hand, perceived irrelevance on the other. (vii) The Applicant's evidence that he lit upon the Tadalafil as the source of the substances when he gratuitously told an employee at a local Max Muscle outlet that he had taken a "sex pill" and she then immediately identified that as the explanation was suspect given that there was no evidence that "sex pills" had ever been previously identified as containing such substances. Mr. Bock indeed suggested that the whole story told by the protagonists lacked the clear ring of truth and had rather the indistinct sound of contrivance.

7.14. However, in the end Mr. Bock was not able to damage the core of the Applicant's explanation. Locker room talk about matters sexual is not an unfamiliar phenomenon. The Panel was ultimately persuaded that it would be an extraordinary coincidence, if the Applicant and Mr. Blasich had sought to contrive a story so as falsely to place the blame for the positive test on the Tadalafil when there was no reason for them to believe or to consider that Tadalafil was contaminated with the prohibited substances, whether purchased in its pure form in prescribed Cialis or bastardised form as sold by All American Peptide. This would, in the Panel's view, be even less likely than the Utah Laboratory being unable to find, despite its presence, tamoxifen in the Sample provided by the Applicant.

7.15.   5. The Panel was therefore constrained to conclude that the Applicant crossed the threshold of probability in establishing the source of the prohibited substances as being the Tadalafil tablet given by Mr. Blasich to the Applicant on the evening of 14th June 2016.

8.   APPLICABLE RULES

8.1.   Clomiphene and letrozole are "Specified Substances" within the meaning of the WADC list and Article 4.2.2 thereof and Article 4.2.2 of the UFC ADP. In consequence the maximum sanction is one year.

8.2.   Accordingly, where within the spectrum from reprimand to one year ineligibility the appropriate sanction for the ADPV falls depends upon the athlete's degree of fault (UFC ADP 10.5.1.1).

8.3.   As in the case of a Specified Substance, the sanction for an anti-doping policy violation caused by the use of a Contaminated Product can range from a reprimand and no period of ineligibility up to a one-year period of ineligibility in a case involving a Specified Substance, depending on the Athlete's degree of fault (UFC ADP 10.5.1.2).

8.4.   Mr. Jacobs contended in his pre-hearing brief that the Panel should make a "separate assessment" of the Applicant's case under each heading because it is likely to "involve a consideration of different factors". USADA contended in its own brief that the "Contaminated Product" rule does not supply any basis for reducing the Athlete's sanction further than the "Specified Substance" rule.

8.5.   The Panel considers that Mr Jacobs is correct in terms of approach. Axiomatically the nature of the care demanded of an athlete may vary according to the nature of the product ingested. A product may, but need not, be both a "Specified Substance" and a "Contaminated Product". The Panel also accepts Mr Jacobs' submission that if the application of Article 10.5.1.1 and 10.5.1.2 in any particular case results in a different conclusion as to appropriate sanction, the Athlete is in principle entitled to the lower of the two.

8.6. However, the Panel considers that the Respondent's attorneys are correct in submitting that in the present case, the Applicant cannot utilise the Contaminated Product rule.

8.7. Mr. Jacobs argued on the basis of US authority that Tadalafil was a "product" and was contaminated in the sense used in WADC and UFC ADP, because its ingredients were not disclosed on the label nor ascertainable by reasonable internet search.

8.8. The issue, however, in the Panels view is not whether Tadalafil is a product per se; it clearly is – but rather whether the draftsman, epitomizing WADA, of that definition could sensibly be taken to have intended it to apply to a product whose label unambiguously discouraged its consumption at all. The Panel rejects such an interpretation of a definition which was designed to assist an athlete faced with a charge of an ADRV or ADPV and could not reasonably be deployed by someone who should never, according to the label, have taken the pill in the first place. A literal must yield to a teleological interpretation. In any event, as Mr. Jacobs acknowledged, failure to heed the warning on the label, is certainly relevant to fault so that on the facts of the present case, the difference between application of the Specified Substance and Contaminated Product provisions dissolves into nothing.

9. FAULT

9.1. Both parties prayed in aid the taxonomy in Cilic v. ITF (CAS 2013/A/2237, "Cilic") in which, inter alia, the CAS panel sought to provide a framework to determine a sanction applicable to a specified substance case which proposed a three-fold division of degrees of fault: (i) considerable fault, (ii) normal degree of fault, and (iii) light degree of fault;[8]

---

[8] Partly paraphrased in Lea v. USADA (CAS 2016/A/4371) as (i) considerable degree of fault; (ii) moderate degree of fault; and (iii) light degree of fault (at para 90)

and to that end consideration of degree of fault from both an objective and a subjective viewpoint.

9.2. The Panel finds that approach helpful[9] but reminds itself that Cilic provides guidelines, not prescriptive rules, and that each case must be considered by reference to its particular facts and circumstances[10].

9.3. Given its conclusion as to source the Panel has to consider the degree of care (or - its opposite - fault) that the Applicant displayed to avoid the risk that the tablet he took was free from prohibited substances.

9.4. Mr. Jacobs played the best hand that he could, but even an advocate of his ability and experience can do nothing, if he lacks cards of any value. Looking at the objective facts, first what is most striking is what the Applicant did not do rather than what he did do. Mr. Jacobs relied on

the fact that the Applicant believed (mistakenly) that he was taking Cialis, a product which he had previously checked with Mr. Kawa, was not on the WADA or UFC prohibited list. Given those premises, Mr. Jacobs submitted, no or scant criticism of the Applicant was warranted. Mr. Jacobs sought to draw an analogy with the facts of Cilic arguing that in Cilic, the Panel accepted that the athlete's mistake was in believing that the ingredient nikethamide (which was banned) was the same as nikotinamid (which was not banned) and found Mr. Cilic's fault on an analysis of the objective factors, therefore to be in the "light" category so that, by alleged parity of reasoning the Applicant's mistake lay in believing that the pill was Cialis; when in fact it was Tadalafil and his fault could be in consequence no heavier than Mr Cilic's.

9.5. Mr. Jacobs, however, started, in the Panel's view, in the wrong place. The source of the Applicant's mistake was that he made no inquiry whatever of Mr. Blasich as to the provenance of his tablets. He simply

---

[9] Notwithstanding that it was in the context of WADC where the breadth of sanction was different and more rigorous
[10] All cases are "very fact specific", Sharapova v ITF CAS 2016/A/4643 ("Sharapova") para 82

took the word of someone whom he hardly knew, and had only met at the training camp, and who definitely had no authority whatsoever to speak to that issue, that they were Cialis.

9.6. The read across to Cilic therefore fails. In Cilic, the athlete asked his mother to purchase some glucose powder. She purchased a packet which contained banned substance. The Cilic panel noted that the athlete did take some precautions (even though they were not enough to prevent the ADRV):

> "a. The Athlete asked his mother to purchase the product from a safe environment, namely a pharmacy.
>
> b. The Athlete's mother did try to ascertain from the pharmacist whether or not the Coramine Glucose would be safe for the Athlete as a competitive tennis player.
>
> c. The Athlete looked at and read the label on the product. He looked for and noted the two ingredients (...)" (Paragraph 85)

9.7. Contrast the Applicant's position. He did not ask Mr. Blasich to purchase the product from a safe environment: he simply asked him for a tablet. In fact, he did not seem to care about where Mr. Blasich got the tablet; but only about what it could do for him in terms of increasing his sexual pleasure. Mr. Blasich himself took no steps to check that the tablet was not, and did not contain, a Prohibited Substance. The Applicant did not look at or read the label on package from which the tablet was taken, something sensibly said in Knauss v. FIS (CAS 2005/A/847) to be "a clear and obvious precaution" (para 7.3.6). He never asked to see the package at all. The mistake he made was not, like Mr. Cilic, to confuse two substances with deceptively similar names. He took what he thought was Cialis because he relied on the untutored statement of his training partner. The fact that, as the Panel accepts, the Applicant was under the impression that the tablet was Cialis which he had been told by his agent was not a Prohibited Substance did not relieve him his duty of diligence to check on what the product that he took without on his own evidence a moment's hesitation was, what it contained and whence it came. The regulations which governed his conduct as a UFC athlete placed the responsibility for what entered into his system fairly and squarely on him.

9.8. Mr. Bock listed a number of aspects of the Applicant's fault when evaluated against his duty to be responsible for what went into his body. He used a prescription medication without proven medical need but rather for purposes of pleasure, and without a prescription (contrary to the general advice of his agent). He did not tell his agent that he intended to take the so-called Cialis, again contrary to the advice of his agent (indeed he did not tell his agent that he had done so until after the positive test). He did no research whatsoever into the nature of what he was taking, notwithstanding its dubious condition, covered as it visibly was in some kind of powder. He could have carried out all the requisite actions to satisfy his duty of diligence without any real difficulty.

9.9. Had he done any of these things, he would have ascertained from its website that All American Peptide, in addition to Tadalafil, sold a number of substances on the WADA Prohibited List in the classes of (S1) Anabolic Agents; (S2) Peptide Hormones, Growth Factors, Related Substances and Mimetics; and (S4) Hormone and Metabolic Modulators. (The list included, indeed on the same page as Tadalafil, clomiphene, letrozole and tamoxifen.) He would also have seen on the label to the package in which the tablet which he took was contained the emphatic warning:

> "TADALAFIL 30 MG x 40
>
> This Product is for CHEMICAL RESEARCH USE ONLY. NOT INTENDED FOR
>
> HUMAN CONSUMPTION/USE. WARNING: If product is ingested accidently contact Poison Control. (...) This product is not a drug, food, or cosmetic and should not be misbranded, misused or mislabelled (sic) as a drug, food or cosmetic. (...)"

Advice replicated elsewhere in the retailer's literature. Failure to recognise these red flags was the consequence of his fundamental fault, the failure to make due inquiry. That failure not excuse his ignorance of these matters: it simply explains it and identifies how serious it was. Even, if, as Mr. Jacobs argued with some force, the warning on the label was mere camouflage, designed by All American Peptide to provide a defence against FDA prosecutions, that of itself should have warned the Applicant, had he troubled to read it, that he was using a product of dubious origin.

9.10. The Panel was ultimately compelled to ask itself not how much more could the Applicant had done, but how much less. It concluded that the Applicant's degree of fault was at the very top end of the scale. In Sharapova exploring the concept of "no significant fault" in WADC, the CAS panel said "an athlete can always read the label of the product used or make Internet searches to ascertain its ingredients, cross-check the ingredients so identified against the Prohibited List or consult with the relevant sporting or anti-doping organizations, consult appropriate experts in anti-doping matters and, eventually, not take the product. However an athlete cannot reasonably be expected to follow all such steps in each and every circumstance. To find otherwise would render the NSF[11] provision in the WADC meaningless" (para 84). The fact that not every such step must always be taken before an athlete can be acquitted of significant or considerable fault does not mean that there is no need to take any such step (as was the case here) in order to achieve such acquittal.

9.11. Mr. Jacobs relied on two other matters. First the fact that the Applicant had delegated his duties to his agent, second that he lacked adequate experience of or education in anti-doping matters.

9.12. As to the first, given that the responsibility to ensure that no prohibited substance is used by him lies upon the athlete, there is a strong case to be made out and one supported by a well-known trend of CAS authority, that an athlete who delegates the fulfilment of that

---

[11] No significant fault - a concept absent from the UFC ADP

responsibility to a delegate is fixed with any fault of that delegate. Sharapova takes a less demanding line. However, there is no need for the Panel to resolve any resulting conflict in the case law or consequent uncertainty. It is content to assume, without holding, that the Sharapova approach is applicable to the present case.

9.13. In Sharapova:

> "(...) the parties agreed before this Panel to follow the approach indicated by Al Nahyan (§ 177), i.e. that athletes are permitted to delegate elements of their anti-doping obligations. If, however, an anti-doping rule violation is committed, the objective fact of the third party's misdeed is imputed to the athlete, but the sanction remains commensurate with the athlete's personal fault or negligence in his/her selection and oversight of such third party, or, alternatively, for his /her own negligence in not having checked or controlled the ingestion of the prohibited substance. In other words, the fault to be assessed is not that which is made by the delegate, but the fault made by the athlete in his/her choice. As a result, as the Respondent put it, a player who delegates his/her anti-doping responsibilities to another is at fault if he/she chooses an unqualified person as her delegate, if he/she fails to instruct him properly or set out clear procedures he/she must follow in carrying out his task, and/or if he/she fails to exercise supervision and control over him/her in the carrying out of the task. The Panel also concurs with such approach."
> (Paragraph 85)

9.13. If this was the correct approach, the Applicant's case is in no way improved. Mr. Kawa was not qualified, whatever his other skills, to advise the Applicant on anti-doping matters. He had no medical or scientific background. He could at most inquire – as he did – from those who were qualified, in this instance Mr. Novitsky, as to whether a particular product or substance was on the banned list. His attitude as to the general counsel he gave the Applicant was bizarre and the reverse of helpful; for example, he said that because he knew that the Applicant did not take steroids, he felt it unnecessary to advise him not to do so. The Applicant gave Mr. Kawa no clear – or any – instruction as to how to perform his task of preventing the Applicant from violating anti-doping rules. The Applicant failed to exercise any supervision as to how Mr. Kawa was performing his task. As the Panel has already noted, having agreed to tell Mr. Kawa about anything he took so that Mr. Kawa could advise him whether he would be compliant with UFC ADP if he took it, on this critical occasion, he failed to do so. Had he told Mr. Kawa the full facts about the product, its packaging, and its provenance, he would surely, have received advice not to take the product at all.

9.14. As to the second, the Panel recognises that the Applicant was not among the cohort of Olympic athletes, and may have had less education on anti-doping matters than they. The issue, however, is whether the education he did have, was enough to enable him to know how to comply with the UFC ADP.

9.15. Panel has seen the tutorial manuals and heard from Mr Novitsky, who influenced their compilation, and concludes that over the 12 months prior to the positive test, the education available to the Applicant was sufficient. The introduction to the Athlete's advantage programme gave basic and easily understandable guidance as to how to avoid infringing the UFC ADP (as well as to whereabouts compliance). The very first module (October 2015) dealt with the prohibited list and sanctions. The December 2015 tutorial repeated the message in equally clear terms. The message of personal responsibility, the need for checking and research, the potential issues with medications and supplements as well as a summary of the major banned substances were all set out.

9.16. The Applicant's fault was in not making use of the available material, but rather in relying on his agent to give what, on Mr. Kawa's own evidence, was an incomplete and inadequate summary.

Furthermore the Applicant allowed his agent or his agent's brother to confirm that he had understood the material in the course when at best he had received the agent's potted version. This was yet another example of the Applicant's casual rather than careful attitude to his responsibilities.

9.17   Nor in this context can the Panel ignore the fact that he had been tested no less than five times prior to 16 June 2016, itself a highly educational experience given the content of the forms he was obliged to complete on each occasion.

9.18   Panel has taken due note of the cases cited by Mr. Jacobs to show that the degree of education – or lack of it – in anti-doping matters is relevant to a fault assessment (Qerimaj v. IWF CAS 2012/A/2822 ("Qerimaj"); Oliveira v. USADA CAS 2010/A/2107 ("Oliveira"); WADA v. Hardy and USADA CAS 2009/A/1870 ("Hardy")) but does not agree that they assist the Applicant. The UFC athlete's advantage program provided "much information" and uttered "stringent warnings" to borrow the vocabulary from Hardy (para 127). The Applicant had the opportunity to consider the information and to heed the warnings. He simply failed to do so. By contrast, Qerimaj never received any education or information in anti-doping matters by his federation or the anti- doping agency of his country (para 8.23). Oliveira likewise had a "lack of any formal anti-doping education" (para 9.34).

10.   . *START DATE*

10.1.   . A timely admission may (but need not necessarily) allow for the period of ineligibility decided upon by a panel to start as early as the sample collection date with consequent benefit to the athlete whose comeback into the sport may be pro tanto sooner.

10.2.   In this case, the Panel cannot find that the Applicant has satisfied the precondition which is a sine qua non of the exercise of such discretion in his favour. He did not admit his violation when confronted with the Utah Laboratories test on his Sample. Further the rationale for a benefit to accrue from a prompt admission is that time and money otherwise attendant upon a full hearing will be saved. That has not happened in this case.

11. PROVISIONAL SUSPENSION

11.1. Both parties agree that the Applicant should be given credit against any period of ineligibility served for the suspension already imposed. Such appears to be required by the UFC ADP rules and the Panel will act accordingly.

12. . AGGRAVATING CIRCUMSTANCES

12.1. . Aggravating circumstances are constituted by three cumulative conditions all of which require to be established. The first requires intent to commit an anti-doping rule violation. While the Respondent reserved its position until conclusion of the evidence, in the event no such case of intent was put to or made against the Applicant and, accordingly, the Respondent did not invite the Panel to make a finding that such circumstances existed. The Panel therefore declines to do so.

13. . CONCLUSION

13.1. . The Panel repeats that the Applicant's fault was at the top end of the scale. In short, the Applicant made an advance enquiry about a product Cialis which he did not take. He made no enquiry at all about the Tadalafil pill which he did take. He simply relied upon his team mate to tell him what it was and how it could enhance sexual pleasure. His degree of fault in fact verged on the reckless. It therefore concludes that the maximum sanction of twelve months subject only to the deduction of the period of suspension served will be consonant with the facts as found. It notes that the maximum penalty for specified substances is half that required by the WADC and cannot be said to infringe any principle of proportionality.

13.2 The Panel does not accept that the previous sanctions imposed on other MMA competitors upon which Mr. Jacobs sought to rely provide any guidance. The cases of Romero and Means, UFC athletes, provided instances of classic contaminated products in the form of dietary supplements, purchased from orthodox outlets, whose labels did not disclose the prohibited substances which each contained, in the former Ibutamoren, in the latter Ostarine. Both athletes accepted a sanction of six months, appropriate for a normal or moderate degree of fault; but in neither case was there an adjudication which explored precisely what steps either might have taken to be code-compliant. In such circumstances neither case is in its key features the same as or even similar to that of the Applicant. They provide no precedent of use to the Panel such that it can plausibly be argued that the sanction selected by the Panel is inconsistent with the sanction in those previous cases; and even if they did so, while consistency as to penalty is good, correctness is better.

14. . EPILOGUE

On the evidence before the Panel, the Applicant is not a drug cheat. He did not know that the tablet he took contained prohibited substances or that those substances had the capacity to enhance sporting performance. However by his imprudent use of what he pungently referred to as a "dick pill" he has not only lost a year of his career but an estimated nine million dollars. This outcome which he admits to be a wake-up call for him should serve as a warning to all others who participate in the same sport.

ON THOSE GROUNDS

The Panel rules that the Applicant's period of ineligibility should be 8 months being 12 months less the period of provisional suspension served since 6 July 2016.

Michael J Beloff QC
Chairman

Lars Halgreen
Arbitrator

Markus Manninen
Arbitrator

Dated: November 6, 2016, Santa Monica

From the Author

MMA Fighters, Outside The Cage & Behind bars

This page left blank intentionally